JB JOSSEY-BASS

■ ■ ■ Janice VanCleave's ■ ■ ■

Super Science Challenges

Hands-On Inquiry Projects for Schools, Science Fairs, or Just Plain Fun!

Janice VanCleave

BICENTENNIAL
1807
WILEY
2007
BICENTENNIAL

John Wiley & Sons, Inc.

This book is printed on acid-free paper. ♾

Published by Jossey-Bass
A Wiley Imprint
989 Market Street, San Francisco, CA 94103-1741
www.josseybass.com

Design and composition by Navta Associates, Inc.

The publisher and the author have made every reasonable effort to insure that the experiments and activities in the book are safe when conducted as instructed but assume no responsibility for any damage caused or sustained while performing the experiments or activities in this book. Parents, guardians, and/or teachers should supervise young readers who undertake the experiments and activities in this book.

Jossey-Bass books and products are available through most bookstores. To contact Jossey-Bass directly call our Customer Care Department within the U.S. at 800-956-7739, outside the U.S. at 317-572-3986, or fax 317-572-4002.

Jossey-Bass also publishes its books in a variety of electronic formats. Some content that appears in print may not be available in electronic books.

Library of Congress Cataloging-in-Publication Data

VanCleave, Janice Pratt.
  [Super sciencechallenges]
  Janice VanCleave's super science challenges : hands-on inquiry projects for schools, science fairs, or just plain fun! / Janice VanCleave.—1st ed.
      p. cm.
  Includes index.
  ISBN 978-0-471-47183-7 (pbk.)
  1. Science—Experiments—Juvenile literature. 2. Scientific recreations—Juvenile literature. 3. Science projects—Juvenile literature. 4. Science—Experiments—Study and teaching (Elementary) 5. Science—Experiments—Study and teaching (Secondary). I. Title. II. Title: Super science challenges.
  Q164.V428 2008
  507.8—dc22

                                                                          2007020614

Printed in the United States of America
first edition

10 9 8 7 6 5 4 3 2 1

This book is dedicated to two special people in my life,
my daughters-in-love,
Tina Ryer
and
Ginger VanCleave.

Contents

■ Biology Challenges

■ Chemistry Challenges

Introduction

This book presents fun science facts and challenges for young people. **Science** is a system of knowledge about the nature of things in the universe. It is the result of observing, questioning, and experimenting to test ideas. A **science challenge** is a science problem that can be solved through investigation.

Responding to a science challenge is like being a detective. It requires that you plan well and carefully collect and analyze information. You may wish to use one of the science challenges in this book to develop a class project or a project for a **science fair** (an organized contest in which science projects are compared and judged based on predetermined criteria).

Select a science challenge that interests you, then start with curiosity and a desire to learn something new. Next, proceed with a purpose and a determination to solve the problem. Even if your selected challenge doesn't turn out exactly as you planned, it is likely that your scientific quest will end with some interesting discoveries.

How to Use This Book

This book will give you information and ideas about many science challenges. You can start at any section of the book, or you can flip through the chapters for a challenge that sounds interesting. Before you start your challenge, read all of the chapter describing it. The format for each chapter is as follows:

- **The Challenge:** A science problem that can be solved through investigation.
- **What You Need to Know:** Science facts about the topic of the chapter and definitions of science terms found in the chapter.
- **How Does _____ Work?** A more thorough, but easy to understand explanation of one of the science terms previously introduced.
- **What Does That Have to Do with _____?** An explanation of how the science term previously presented and explained relates to the chapter's challenge.
- **Fun Facts:** Interesting facts related to the challenge topic.
- **Real-Life Science Challenge:** A description of how the chapter topic was used to solve a real-life science problem.
- **Experiment:** Hints to help you solve the challenge through experimentation.

How to Start a Challenge

When designing an experiment to solve a science challenge, you want to consider the variables involved. A **variable** is anything that can change on its own or be changed by you. When experimenting, you want to determine how one variable affects another. For example, if the challenge is to determine the effect of temperature on seed germination, temperature is the **independent variable** (the variable you change) and seed germination is the **dependent variable** (the variable you are observing for changes). To make sure that only temperature causes any observed changes, you must try to keep all other variables constant. The amount of water, light, and type of seeds are some of the variables that might affect the results. It is important not to allow variables to change. Variables other than the independent variable and the dependent variable that are not allowed to change are called **controlled variables**.

When experimenting, it is best to do multiple trials. This gives you more data to confirm your results. **Data** is collected and recorded information. A **control** is an experiment that is used as a standard with which to compare your results. For an experiment that compares the effect of temperature on seed germination, the control can be what you consider the normal temperature at which the seeds would germinate. It could also be the **median** (the middle number in a set of numbers) temperature. All results would be compared to the control. How do seeds germinate at temperatures higher and lower than that of the control temperature?

Safety

Safety is important to all scientists. To make sure the experiments you design are safe, a parent or other adult should supervise all of them.

For Teachers

The challenges in this book are meant to extend students' critical and creative thinking abilities in the context of the science concepts being studied. Each challenge is intended to give students a chance to investigate an area of interest in greater depth than is possible in most science curriculums. A science challenge encourages independent study and accommodates diversity in student learning. The solution to a science challenge is discovered using the inquiry approach.

■ Science Inquiry

The tool for the science inquiry approach is the **scientific method**. This method is the process of identifying a problem, thinking through its possible solution, and designing an experiment to test the possible solution. The scientific method involves the following: **research** (the process of collecting data about a topic being studied); a **problem** (a scientific question to be solved or a scientific purpose to be demonstrated); a **hypothesis** (an idea about the solution to a problem, based on knowledge and research); an **experiment** (the process of testing a hypothesis, answering a scientific question, or demonstrating a scientific purpose); and a **conclusion** (a summary of the results of an experiment and how they relate to the hypothesis or how they solve the challenge problem).

While the steps of the scientific method are listed in a specific order, scientists do not always follow this order. Research is listed as the first step in the scientific method, but research is an ongoing part of any investigation. Challenges are designed to help students develop the skills of asking questions (or posing a problem); predicting what they expect to observe (or forming a hypothesis); planning and conducting investigations (including experiments to test their hypotheses); collecting observations (data); and organizing, examining, and evaluating data by constructing tables, graphs, charts, and maps and drawing conclusions by comparing their hypotheses (expected observations) with their data (actual observations).

■ Assessment

The assessment of student records as well as performance assessment should be the basis of determining how much the student learned. Performance assessment includes the student's ability to carry out physical processes, such as measurement, observation, experimental design, and problem solving, and the student's level of thinking and reasoning skills, including choosing appropriate methods and drawing valid conclusions.

PART I

Astronomy Challenges

Make a Scale Model of the Planets of the Solar System That Shows the Planets' Distances from the Sun

■ **What You Need to Know**

A **model** is a physical representation of something. A **scale model** is a model made using a ratio between the measurements of the model and the measurements of the object that the model represents. **Celestial bodies** are natural bodies in the sky, including stars and planets. A **star** is made of hot gases that give off energy, including heat and light. **Planets orbit** (move in a curved path around another object) a star called a **sun** and shine by reflecting the sun's light. A **solar system** is a group of celestial bodies that orbit a sun. Our solar system has eight official planets in the following order from the **Sun**: Mercury, Venus, Earth, Mars, Jupiter, Saturn, Uranus, and Neptune. (Pluto is classified as a dwarf planet.)

■ **How Does a Scale Model Work?**

In a scale ratio, the measured size of the model comes first. If the first value of the ratio is smaller than the second value, the scale model is smaller than the real object. For example, for the scale model of Earth's layers on page 10, a scale ratio of 1 cm : 1,000 km is used. This means that 1 cm on the model is equal to 1,000 km on the real object, the Earth. The scale ratio can be written as 1 cm/1,000 km, which means 1 cm ÷ 1,000 km. The following formula is used to determine the measurements for the model:

Model Distance	= Actual distance × scale ratio.
Core Diameter	= 6,800 km × 1 cm ÷ 1,000 km
	= 6.8 cm
Mantle Depth	= 2,900 km × 1 cm ÷ 1,000 km
	= 2.9 cm

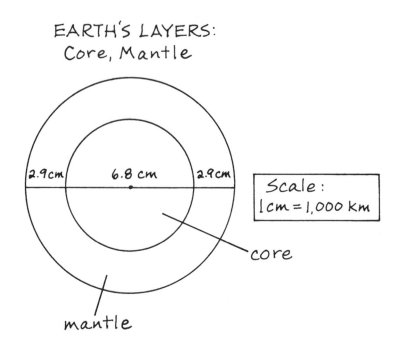

EARTH'S LAYERS:
Core, Mantle

2.9cm   6.8 cm   2.9cm

Scale:
1cm = 1,000 km

core

mantle

What Does This Have to Do with Comparing Planet Distances?

PLANET DISTANCE FROM THE SUN	
Planet	**Distance from the Sun in AU**
Mercury	0.4
Venus	0.7
Earth	1
Mars	1.5
Jupiter	5.2
Saturn	9.5
Uranus	19.2
Neptune	30.1

Because the distances between the planets are so large, a scale model must be used to make a visual comparison between them. To determine the scale for your model, first look at the largest and smallest measurements. Your model must be able to represent both measurements. For example, as you can see from the table on this page, Mercury has the shortest distance from the Sun of 0.4 AU and Neptune the longest distance of 30.1 AU. If a scale of 1 cm : 1 AU is used, the model distance for Mercury would be 0.4 cm (0.4 AU × 1 cm ÷ 1 AU) and the model distance for Neptune would be 30.1 cm (30.1 AU × 1 cm ÷ 1 AU). Are these measurements going to work for your model? If not, you'll have to scale your model up or down.

Fun Fact

The average distance of Earth from the Sun is about 93 million miles (149 million km). Astronomers call this distance 1 AU (an **astronomical unit**) and use this to measure distances within the solar system. If you rode in a spacecraft traveling at 100 miles per hour (1,600 kph), it would take over 100 years for you to travel a distance equal to 1 AU. The unit used by astronomers to measure distances outside the solar system is the light-year. One **light-year** is the distance that light will travel in 1 year, which is about 63,000 AU.

Real-Life Science Challenge

Why do scale models of the solar system generally represent planet distances or planet sizes, but not both? This is because of the great differences between the two measurements. The scale of 1 cm : 1 AU can be used to represent Mercury, with the least distance on the model of 0.4 cm, and Neptune, with the greatest distance of 30.1 cm. But if the same scale is used for planet sizes, Mercury, with the smallest diameter, would be only 0.0000327 cm in diameter, and Jupiter, the largest planet, would be only 0.00097 cm in diameter. These measurements are too small to make with ordinary rulers and are too small to see with the unaided eye. On the other hand, if you made the planet models large enough to show their relative sizes clearly, you would have to space them out to very large distances. For example, if Mercury is 0.5 cm in diameter and Jupiter is 14.7 cm in diameter, the distance of Mercury from the Sun on the model would have to be 5,945 km and the distance from the Sun to Jupiter would have to be 79,746 km. Neptune, the farthest planet, would have to be 460,845 km away. There are about 1,600 km in 1 mile.

Experiment

Now, start experimenting with designs for your solar system model.

Hints

- ☐ Using the distances shown in the table on page 10 try making scales using different units.
- ☐ Decide on the materials you will use for your model, such as posterboard, Styrofoam, or clay for the planets, and how the model will be displayed.
- ☐ Measure carefully when building your model, and don't forget to label your scale.

CHALLENGE

2

ASTRONOMY

Demonstrate How the Sun Appears in Different Parts of the Sky during the Year

■ **What You Need to Know**

The Earth orbits the Sun and rotates. **Rotation** is the spinning of an object about its **axis**, which is an imaginary line through the center of the object. During these Earth movements, the Sun and the stars are relatively stationary as Earth orbits the Sun. But from Earth, it appears that the Sun and the stars rise above the eastern **horizon** (the line where the Earth and sky appear to meet), move across the sky, and set below the western horizon. If the stars could be seen during the day, it would appear that they move faster than the sun. The **ecliptic**, which is the apparent path of the Sun across the sky, traces an imaginary circle around Earth. The ecliptic runs through the **zodiac**, which is an 18° wide band of the sky, 9° above and 9° below the ecliptic.

The zodiac is divided into twelve parts called **signs**. Each sign is a patch of sky 30° wide and 18° high. A **sun sign** is the sign of the zodiac the Sun rises with at dawn. There are 12 signs, and each is associated with a **constellation** (a group of stars that appear to form a pattern in the sky) called a **zodiac constellation**. The name of

ZODIAC CONSTELLATIONS			
Name	**Pronunciation**	**Name**	**Pronunciation**
Aries, the Ram	AIR-eez	Libra, the Scales	LEE-bruh
Taurus, the Bull	TOR-us	Scorpius, the Scorpion	SKOR-pee-us
Gemini, the Twins	JEH-muh-nye	Sagittarius, the Archer	sa-juh-TAIR-ee-us
Cancer, the Crab	KAN-sur	Capricornus, the Sea Goat	ka-prih-KOR-nus
Leo, the Lion	LEE-oh	Aquarius, the Water Bearer	uh-KWAIR-ee-us
Virgo, the Maiden	VUR-go	Pisces, the Fish	PYE-seez

each sign is the name of the zodiac constellation in it. The zodiac constellations are listed in the chart below.

How Do Sun Signs Work?

In the diagram, position 1 shows Earth, the Sun, and the constellation Pisces at dawn. The Sun is in the sign called Pisces, but the Sun's brightness prevents the stars making up the Pisces constellation from being seen at dawn. Nevertheless, for about 30 days some or all of the stars of Pisces are behind the Sun at dawn.

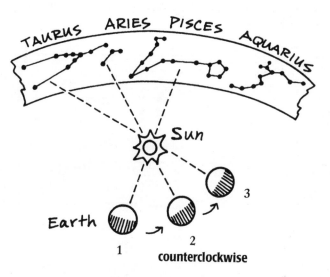

What Does This Have to Do with the Sun Moving to Different Parts of the Sky?

Because Earth revolves around the Sun, from Earth it appears that the Sun moves counterclockwise from one zodiac sign to the next during the year. This means that the Sun appears to move from Pisces to Aries, then to Taurus, and so on. Actually, Earth is moving from position 1 to position 2, then to position 3, and so on.

Real-Life Science Challenge

What is the difference between astronomy and astrology? **Astrology** is the notion that the positions and motions of the stars and planets determine people's personalities and influence the course of their daily lives. **Astronomy** is the scientific study of celestial bodies. Because astrology does not use scientific methods to reach its conclusions, it is considered a **pseudoscience**.

Experiment

Now, start experimenting to demonstrate how the Sun is seen in different parts of the sky during the year.

Hints

- ☐ Use a curved piece of cardboard to represent the zodiac band and Styrofoam balls to represent the Sun and Earth.
- ☐ Design a way to represent Earth orbiting the Sun.
- ☐ Design a way to point out the Sun sign for each position of Earth during its orbit.
- ☐ Since the stars cannot be seen during the day, design a way to determine the nighttime constellations during different sun signs.

Fun Fact

Horoscopes are predictions or advice for the future of a person based on the position of planets and signs at a specific time. Your horoscope would be for your birth sign, which is the sign the Sun was in when you were born. Birth signs are determined by dates, which were established thousands of years ago. For example, the birth sign for birthdays from February 19 through March 20 is Pisces. But since birth sign dates were established, Earth's axis has changed position. Babies born on February 25 would have a birth sign of Pisces according to **astrologers** (people who predict the future using the position of celestial bodies), but their true sun sign would be Aquarius.

Demonstrate Why Stars of the Same Luminosity Can Appear to Be of Different Brightness

■ **What You Need to Know**

Luminous means giving off light, and **luminosity** is a measure of how much light-energy is given off by something, such as a star. **Apparent magnitude** is the measure of a celestial body's **apparent brightness**, or how bright a celestial object appears to be as observed from Earth.

■ **How Does Apparent Magnitude Work?**

Over 2,000 years ago, the Greek astronomer Hipparchus of Nicaea (c. 190–120 B.C.) designed a number system for ranking stars according to their apparent brightness. The brightest stars were assigned magnitude 1; the faintest stars that can be seen with the unaided eye (that is, under perfect viewing conditions) were assigned magnitude 6. The diagram below of the constellation Aries, the Ram, shows the magnitudes of the stars in parentheses. As indicated by their lower numbers, the stars Hamal and Sheratan are brighter than Mesarthim.

On the modern apparent magnitude scale, a first-magnitude star is exactly 100 times brighter than a sixth-magnitude star. The modern scale also measures magnitudes greater than 6 and less than 1. The larger the scale number, the dimmer the star. For example, a star with a magnitude of 9 is much dimmer than one with a magnitude of 7. Scale numbers less than 0 are negative. The higher the negative number, the brighter the star. For example, a star with a magnitude of –2 is brighter than a star with a magnitude of –1 or of +2.

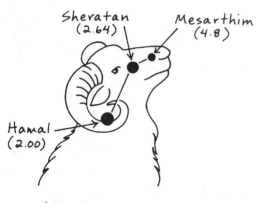

ARIES, THE RAM

Fun Fact

The Sun, with a magnitude of −26.8, is the brightest light in the sky. The Moon and the planets are not luminous. Instead, they reflect the Sun's light. A full moon has an apparent magnitude of −12.6, and the planet Venus, at −4.5, has the greatest apparent magnitude of the rest of the celestial bodies.

The diagram below shows how light spreads from a source and how bright a light spot would appear at different distances from the source. Each light spot has the same number of lines (six), indicating that the three lights have the same luminosity. The brightness of each light spot is indicated by how spread out the light is. The more the light is spread out, as indicated by the distance between the lines in the spot, the dimmer the light source will appear. In other words, as the distance from the light source increases, the less bright it appears. Because the higher the apparent magnitude number the dimmer the light, an increase in distance from Earth increases a star's apparent magnitude.

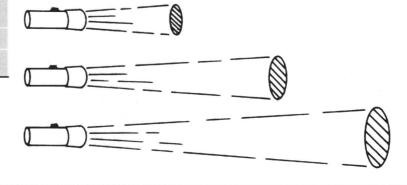

Real-Life Science Challenge

The dimmest celestial bodies visible by the human eye under perfectly dark skies are around magnitude +6. With the aid of the **Hubble space telescope** (a telescope in orbit around the Earth), celestial bodies with a magnitude of +30 can be seen. The Hubble space telescope allows astronomers to view objects at a distance of 60 million light-years.

Experiment

Now, design an experiment to demonstrate how stars with the same luminosity can have different apparent magnitudes.

Hints

- Use identical flashlights to represent stars with the same luminosity.
- Design a way to measure the brightness of luminous bodies from different distances.

4

ASTRONOMY

Determine Which Light Color Has the Least Effect on Night Vision

■ What You Need to Know

Optical instruments are devices, such as telescopes, designed to aid human vision. The **light-gathering power** of optical instruments is the amount of light the instrument can collect. **Light amplification** is the process by which objects viewed through an optical instrument appear brighter than when viewed with the unaided eye. The **aperture** of an optical instrument is the opening through which light enters. The aperture size indicates the light-gathering power of the instrument. The pupils of your eyes have a variable (changing) aperture. They **contract** (get smaller) in the light and **dilate** (get larger) in the dark. In the light, your eye is said to be **light-adapted** and in the dark it is **dark-adapted**, also called night vision.

■ How Does Dark-Adaptation Work?

The aperture of your eye is the pupil. White light causes your pupils to contract or get smaller, restricting the amount of light that enters the eye. This is called having light-adapted eyes. In the dark your pupils dilate or get larger, which allows more light to enter. This is called having dark-adapted eyes. Your pupils are like the aperture of a telescope: the larger the aperture, the more light-gathering power. This is important when studying the night sky. With a larger aperture or pupil, your eyes can gather more starlight so you can see more stars.

Dark-adapted
(Large aperture)

Light-adapted
(Small aperture)

What Does This Have to Do with Colored Light?

While studying the night sky, astronomers may need to read star maps and/or take notes without losing their night vision. Would colored light have less effect on night vision than white light? Would the shades of the different colors have any effect?

Real-Life Science Challenge

There are two kinds of light-detecting cells on the back of your eye: **cones** and **rods**. The cones occupy a small spot centrally located on the back of your eye, and the rods surround the cones and cover a much greater area. When you look straight ahead, light enters your eyes and falls on the cones, which are cells for high-level light that specialize in color perception. When you look to the side (up, down, left, or right), light enters your eyes and falls mostly on the rods, which are sensitive to low-level light. Astronomers have discovered that when viewing objects with low-level light the best view is achieved by looking off to the side. This is because the light falls on the rods instead of the cones. This method of viewing is called **averted vision**.

Experiment

Now, start experimenting with colored lights and night vision.

Hints

- □ A flashlight can be used as a light source.
- □ Colored transparent cellophane or plastic report folders can be used over the white light source to produce colored light.
- □ Design a way to measure the degree of change each type of light makes to dark-adapted eyes.

Fun Fact

Having dark-adapted eyes is called having night vision. When you move from a lighted area to a dark area, at first you can hardly see. After a few minutes, changes occur in your eyes and you can see better. In about 30 minutes to an hour, the changes are complete and your vision is even better. Although your vision is not as good as in the light, it is the best it will be in the dark. You now have night vision.

One flash of white light, such as from a flashlight, instantly changes dark-adapted eyes to light-adapted eyes. But turning off the light doesn't instantly change the eyes back to their dark-adapted state. It takes another 30 minutes to an hour to get back your night vision.

CHALLENGE 5

ASTRONOMY

Determine How the Focal Length of a Magnifying Lens Affects Its Magnifying Power

■ **What You Need to Know**

A **lens** is a curved piece of **transparent** (see-through) material, such as glass or plastic. The shape of the lens changes the direction of the path of light passing through it. If the lens has two curved sides it is called a **double lens**. If it has one curved side it is called a **single lens**. A **convex lens** has a surface that curves outward like the surface of a ball. This type of lens is thicker at the center than at the edge. A magnifying lens is an example of a **double convex lens**. The line passing through the center of any lens is called the **principal axis**. Any convex lens, single or double, causes light rays that are **parallel** (equally distant apart) to its principal axis to **refract** (bend or change direction) as they pass through the lens and meet on the axis. The point where the light rays meet is called the **focal point**. The **focal length** is the distance from the lens to the focal point. The **magnifying power** of a lens is the number of times it can make the size of the image greater than the size of the object being viewed.

■ **How Does a Lens Work?**

As parallel light rays pass through a convex lens, they are refracted toward the center of the lens. The light is refracted as it enters the lens and again when it exits the lens. As shown in the diagram on page 20, the refracted rays are focused, meaning they come together at one point called the focal point. The amount of refraction depends on how curved the lens is. The more curved a lens, the greater is its refraction and the shorter its focal length.

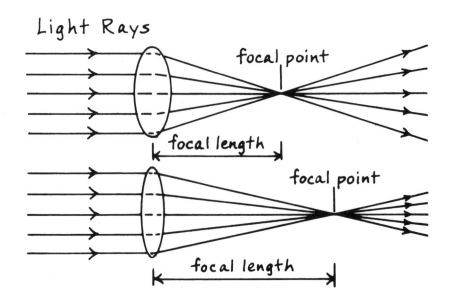

Light Rays

focal point

focal length

focal point

focal length

■ What Does This Have to Do with Magnifying Power?

The magnifying power (M_p) of a lens is equal to the average distance of distinct vision (D_a) of most people divided by the focal length (D_f) of the lens. This relationship expressed as a word formula is:

magnifying power = average distance of
distinct vision ÷ focal length

This relationship expressed as a symbol equation is:

$$M_p = D_a \div D_f$$

For example, a lens with a 5× magnifying power will magnify an object so that it appears five times the size it would appear at the average distance of distinct vision.

Real-Life Science Challenge

Scientists continue to be challenged to invent microscopes that reveal the hidden world of atomic structures. A **scanning probe microscope (SPM)** is a type of computerized microscope that allows scientists to study the atoms on the surface of a material. In an SPM, a probe scans the surface of a material. The movements of the probe are picked up by a computer and sent to a screen where an image of the surface appears.

■ Experiment

Now, design an experiment to compare the magnifying power of two or more lenses with different focal lengths.

Hints

☐ Determine how to measure the focal length of a lens.

☐ Determine the average distance of distinct vision for a particular object.

☐ Calculate the magnifying power of each lens.

Fun Fact

The Dutch scientist Antoni van Leeuwenhoek (1632–1723), who designed some of the first microscopes, prepared his own magnifying lenses. With them, he studied everything from blood to scrapings from the teeth of an old man who claimed never to have cleaned his teeth. It is not surprising that he found tiny moving creatures in the old man's teeth scrapings. He called these critters animalcules. We now call them **microorganisms**.

Use the North Star to Determine Where You Live on Earth

■ **What You Need to Know**

Since **altitude** is the distance in degrees above the horizon, the altitude of the horizon is 0°. A point directly overhead in the sky is called the **zenith**. The altitude of the zenith is 90°.

■ **How Does Altitude Work?**

To an observer on Earth, the visible sky appears to be a dome over Earth with stars and other celestial bodies on it. The measurement from any point on the horizon to the zenith is 90°. Celestial bodies in the sky located between the horizon and the zenith have an altitude between 0° and 90°. For example, the star shown in the diagram below is halfway between the horizon and the zenith, thus its altitude is 45°.

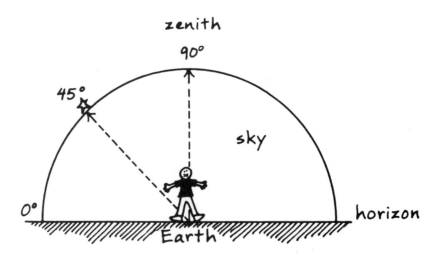

What Does That Have to Do with Where You Live on the Earth?

The North Star, **Polaris**, is the only star in the sky that appears not to move. So the altitude of this star is always the same from a specific location on Earth, such as your home. For observers in the Northern Hemisphere, the altitude of the North Star is equal to the latitude of the observer. How can you show this?

Fun Fact

If you could stand at the North Pole, you would have to look straight up to see Polaris. At this location, Polaris is at its highest point in the sky. As you travel south toward the equator, the star appears lower in the sky. It would be at the horizon at the equator, and it is not visible south of the equator.

Real-Life Science Challenge

How did Christopher Columbus find his way across the ocean? Columbus, as well as sailors living before him, used Polaris to determine his northward and southward direction. If sailors wanted to travel in a straight line across the ocean, the altitude of Polaris would have to remain constant throughout their journey. To change to a more northerly course, Polaris would need to be higher in the sky, and it would have to be lower in the sky for a more southerly course.

Experiment

Now, start experimenting with different ways to measure the altitude of the North Star above your home. Compare your measurements to your home's latitude.

Hints

☐ Use a map with latitude lines or look online to determine the latitude of your home.

☐ Use a star map to locate Polaris.

☐ Design a way to measure the altitude of Polaris.

Design a Way to Measure Parallax Shift and Use It to Determine the Distance to an Object

■ **What You Need to Know**

The apparent change in position of an object when viewed from two different points is called **parallax shift**. The distance between the two points is the **baseline**.

■ **How Does Parallax Shift Work?**

Hold your thumb at arm's length in front of you. Close your right eye and look at your thumb with your left eye. Notice how your thumb lines up with the distant objects behind your thumb. Without moving your thumb, close your left eye and open your right eye. Again, look at your thumb. Your will notice a change in

the objects behind your thumb. This apparent change in the position of your thumb in relation to the distant object is parallax shift.

What Does This Have to Do with Measuring Distance?

Parallax shift can be used to determine the distance to an object using the following formula:

$$d = 57.3° \times \text{baseline distance} \div \text{parallax shift}$$

When the baseline distance is divided by the parallax shift, the answer is a number without a unit. To express the answer in degrees, the number is multiplied by 57.3°. The smaller the parallax shift, the farther away the object is. For example, if the baseline is 2 inches, an object with a parallax shift of 5° is closer than an object with a parallax shift of 10°.

$$d = 57.3° \times 2 \text{ inches } (5 \text{ cm}) \div 5°$$
$$= 2.292 \text{ inches } (5.73 \text{ cm})$$
$$d = 57.3° \times 2 \text{ inches } (5 \text{ cm}) \div 10°$$
$$= 1.146 \text{ inches } (2.865 \text{ cm})$$

Real-Life Science Challenge

When Sedna was discovered in 2003, scientists were challenged to determine if it was part of our solar system, meaning that it orbits the Sun. On March 16, 2004, the Hubble telescope took 35 pictures of Sedna. When scientists looked at the pictures in order, Sedna appeared to move slightly, indicating a parallax shift, which demonstrated to scientists that it was a member of the solar system.

Fun Fact

Our solar system no longer has nine planets. Pluto continues to be part of the solar system, but it has been demoted from a regular planet to a dwarf planet. This came about because of the discovery of Sedna, a celestial body that is smaller than Pluto but that, like Pluto, orbits the Sun. Astronomers decided that if Pluto and Sedna were called planets, then asteroids orbiting the Sun should also be called planets.

Now, start experimenting with ways to measure parallax shift and use it to determine the distance to an object.

Hints

☐ You could use a pencil eraser to represent the object whose distance is being measured.

☐ You could draw stars on a piece of paper and secure it to a wall to represent distant stars.

☐ The farther away the background objects are, the greater the parallax shift will be.

☐ Design a way to change the length of the baseline.

Determine Why the Sun and the Moon Appear to Be the Same Size in the Sky

■ What You Need to Know

Apparent size is how large an object appears to be from a specific distance. An object's **actual size** is its true measurement.

■ How Does Apparent Size Work?

The actual size of an object, such as a car, is its true measurement. When you stand next to the car, the car is much bigger than you are. When the car moves away from you, it looks smaller than it really is. An object's apparent size decreases as the object's distance from you increases.

■ What Does This Have to Do with the Size of the Sun and the Moon?

Viewed from Earth, celestial bodies, such as the Sun and the Moon, appear to be much smaller than their actual size. The greater their distance from Earth, the smaller their apparent size compared to their actual size. In order for two celestial bodies of different sizes to have the same apparent size, the ratio between their diameter and their distance from Earth must be equal. The ratio for their distances can be written as: D_{sun}/D_{moon}. The ratio for their diameters can be written as: d_{sun}/d_{moon}. A formula representing the comparison for the two ratios is:

$$D_{sun}/D_{moon} = d_{sun}/d_{moon}$$

Real-Life Science Challenge

Because the Sun and the Moon, as seen from Earth, have the same apparent size, the German scientist Albert Einstein (1879–1955) proved that **gravity** (the force of attraction between all objects in the universe) bends light rays. He predicted that a star positioned behind the Sun would be visible during a total eclipse. This is because the gravity of the Sun would cause the light rays coming from the star to change direction and make the star appear to be next to the Sun. Einstein's prediction was proven correct during a total solar eclipse in 1919.

■ **Experiment**

Now, start experimenting with the relationship between the Sun and the Moon's size and their distance from Earth.

Fun Fact

Since the Moon orbits Earth, sometimes it comes between Earth and the Sun. Because the Sun and the Moon appear to be the same size when viewed from Earth, the Moon can block the Sun completely. When this happens, it is called a **total solar eclipse**. The region from which a total solar eclipse is visible, called the **path of totality**, is very narrow. Few people have seen a total solar eclipse.

Hints

☐ Find the diameters of Earth and the Sun.

☐ Paper disks can be used to model the diameters of the Moon and the Sun.

☐ Find the actual distances of the Moon and the Sun from the Earth.

☐ Create a scale model (see chapter 1) to place Moon and Sun models at appropriate distances from an observer on Earth.

☐ Use the formulas above to compare the ratios of the Sun's and the Moon's diameters and their distances from Earth.

Demonstrate How Earth's Rotation Affects Launching a Rocket into Space

What You Need to Know

Rotation is the spinning of an object about its **axis**, which is an imaginary line through the center of the object. **Velocity** is the speed of an object in a certain direction. **Escape velocity** is how fast an object must travel to escape the pull of gravity (the force that pulls things toward the center of the Earth) in order to be launched into space.

How Does Escape Velocity Work

When you throw a ball up it falls back to Earth. This is because gravity causes the ball to continue to slow until it stops its upward movement, then it starts falling back to Earth. If you throw the ball harder, it starts off with a greater velocity and will go higher before gravity causes it to stop. How hard would you have to throw a ball to prevent it from falling back to Earth? The answer is that the ball must be thrown hard enough so that its velocity is great enough that gravity cannot bring it to a stop. This starting velocity is called escape velocity.

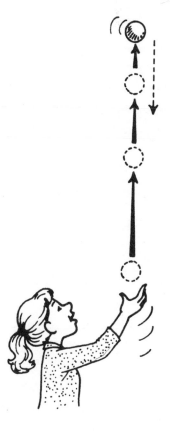

You are sitting in a convertible and throw a ball out the window. The ball is thrown with a force so that the velocity of the ball is 20 miles (32 km) per hour. However, if the car is moving at 50 miles (80 km) per hour north and you throw the same ball with the same force, the velocity of the ball will depend on the direction you throw it. If it is thrown in the same direction the car is moving, the ball's velocity will be the sum of the velocity of the car and the velocity of the ball, which is 70 miles (112 km) per hour north. But if the ball is thrown in the opposite direction from the one the car is moving, the ball's velocity will be the difference between the velocity of the car and the ball, which is 30 miles (48 km) per hour north. Because the car is going faster than the ball is being thrown, the ball will still be traveling in the same direction as the car, only slower. Earth's rotation has the same effect on the speed and direction of rockets launched from its surface.

Fun Fact

Contrary to popular belief, Earth's rotation does not cause water draining from sinks and bathtubs to spin differently in the Northern and Southern Hemispheres. Instead, the water spins in a direction determined by several factors, such as the shape of the sink or the tub and the way in which the water is moving before the drain is opened.

Real-Life Science Challenge

One of the biggest challenges of space travel is for spacecrafts to achieve escape velocity. It takes an enormous amount of fuel for the spacecraft to move fast enough to break away from Earth's gravitational pull. The fuel adds weight to the spacecraft, and when an object is heavier, it takes more energy to lift it. To create more energy, you need more fuel. Scientists are working on ideas for lighter vehicles, more efficient fuels, and new methods for producing the needed energy to achieve escape velocity.

■ Experiment

Now, start designing ways to demonstrate how rotation affects launching a rocket.

Hints

☐ You could use a merry-go-round to represent the rotating Earth and a small beanbag to represent a rocket.

☐ Design a way to launch the beanbag.

☐ Measure how far the beanbag travels when it is launched in the direction of rotation and when it is launched in the opposite direction.

Determine How the Positions of the Sun, the Moon, and Earth Affect Moon Phases

■ **What You Need to Know**

A **moon phase** is one of the repeating shapes of the sunlit surface of the Moon as seen from Earth. A **lunar month** is the time between two successive and similar moon phases, which is about 29½ days. The **waxing** period of a lunar month is the time when the visible lighted surface of the Moon gets bigger. The **waning** period of a lunar month follows the waxing period and is the time when the visible lighted surface of the Moon gets smaller.

■ **How Do Moon Phases Work?**

The Moon's shape appears to change from day to day. These changes in the Moon's apparent shape are called moon phases. Phases are seen because the Moon orbits around Earth. Just as half of the Earth has daylight and the other half nighttime, half of the Moon is lit by the Sun while the other half is not. The phases of the Moon depend on how much of the sunlit half can be seen from Earth at any one time. The waxing moon phases are: new moon, crescent moon, first quarter moon, gibbous moon, full moon. The **new moon** is the phase when the side of the Moon facing Earth is not lit. The **full moon** is the phase when the side of the Moon facing Earth is fully lit.

Following the full moon, the Moon goes through the same phases in reverse. These phases are said to be **waning** (getting smaller). The phases in the waning period are full moon, gibbous moon, third quarter moon, and crescent moon. Then the cycle begins again with the new moon.

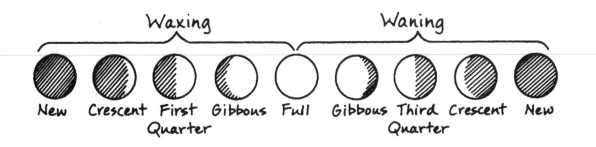

Waxing | Waning

New — Crescent — First Quarter — Gibbous — Full — Gibbous — Third Quarter — Crescent — New

■ What Does This Have to Do with the Position of the Sun, Earth, and the Moon?

The position of the Moon relative to the Sun changes daily. When the Moon is between Earth and the Sun, we see a new moon. When the Moon is opposite the Sun and Earth is in between, we see a full moon. When the Moon is in between these two positions, different fractions of the lit side are seen.

Fun Fact

A full moon occurs about 12.3 times each year. As a result, some months have two full moons. This occurs about every 2.75 years. The second full moon that occurs during one month is called a **blue moon**. The saying "once in a blue moon" means something that happens very seldom. About every 19 years, a year will have two blue moons.

Real-Life Science Challenge

Because only one side of the Moon faces Earth, does the Moon have what some people call a "dark side"? We see only one side of the Moon because it circles Earth in the same amount of time it takes to rotate on its axis. But while the same side always faces us, the Sun shines on all parts of the Moon's face at different times. The side of the Moon that we never see is more accurately called the "far side."

■ Experiment

Now, start experimenting with a way to demonstrate the position of the Sun, the Moon, and Earth at different moon phases.

Hints

☐ Try using a light of some kind, such as a flashlight or a lamp, to represent the Sun.

☐ Use different-size Styrofoam balls to represent Earth and the Moon.

PART II

Biology Challenges

Determine How the Concentration of a Salt Solution Affects the Rate of Osmosis

What You Need to Know

A **solution** is a liquid containing dissolved substances. The liquid part is called a **solvent** and the dissolved part is called the **solute**. The **concentration** of a solution is the amount of dissolved solute in a solvent. **Dissolving** is the process of the solute breaking apart and thoroughly mixing with the solvent. **Osmosis** is the movement of water through a **membrane** (a thin bendable sheet of material) from an area of low solute concentration to an area of high solute concentration.

How Does Osmosis Work?

To understand how osmosis works, it helps to think of the individual particles in a solution, such as a mixture of water (the solvent) and salt (the solute). A solution that contains very few dissolved salt particles has a low salt (solute) concentration. This means that most of the solution is water. The opposite is true if the solution contains many dissolved salt particles.

If vegetables, such as slices of celery, are placed in a bowl of plain water, they become plumper and crisper. This is because water moves into the celery cells due to osmosis. The water moves through the membrane surrounding the celery cells from the side with the lowest salt concentration (plain water) to the side with the

higher salt concentration (the solution inside the celery cells). With an increased amount of water in the celery's cells, the celery pieces become crisper, meaning they are firmer. This firmness of the cell resulting from pressure of its contents on the cell membrane is called **turgor**.

What Does This Have to Do with the Rate of Osmosis?

The **rate of osmosis** is a measure of the amount of water that moves through a membrane in a certain amount of time.

Real-Life Science Challenge

Reverse osmosis is the opposite of osmosis. This means that water is forced to move from a solution of high solute concentration through a membrane to a solution of low solute concentration. This separates water from the solute, which is left behind. Reverse osmosis is used to remove water during the process of changing maple **sap** (a watery solution in plants with dissolved nutrients) to maple syrup. Another use of reverse osmosis is to remove water from dissolved impurities.

Experiment

Now, start experimenting with osmosis.

Hints
☐ Make solutions with different salt concentrations.
☐ Determine a method of testing turgor pressure.
☐ Observe the amount of turgor pressure in a plant, such as celery, at different times, to determine the rate of osmosis.

Fun Fact

Slugs are pests for any gardener. They eat a wide variety of plants, causing anything from slight damage to the death of the plant. The cells of slugs, like all living cells, are surrounded by a membrane. If salt touches a slug, the salt dissolves in the water that lies on the animal's skin. This results in a higher salt concentration outside the slug than inside. Water quickly leaves the cells, resulting in the slug appearing to melt. If enough water is lost, the slug will die.

While salt will kill slugs, it can also kill plants. Other methods of controlling slugs include placing barriers around plants that slugs do not like to cross, such as eggshells and sawdust.

Create a Test to Determine if People Favor One Foot over the Other

■ **What You Need to Know**

Your **dominant** body parts are the ones that you use most.

■ **How Does a Dominant Body Part Work?**

Generally, one hand (right or left) will feel more comfortable performing actions, such as throwing or catching a ball, writing, or using a fork. If you always or almost always use your right hand, then this is your dominant hand, and you are said to be "right-handed." If you generally use your left hand, you are "left-handed." Some people can use either hand with equal ease, so they are **ambidextrous**.

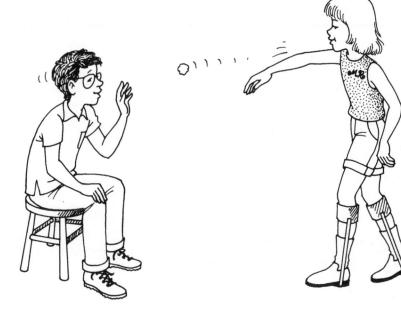

What Does This Have to Do with Your Favorite Foot?

Just as some people have a favorite hand, they can also have a favorite foot. Instead of the word favorite, scientists call it you dominant hand or foot. When you start walking, you generally step forward with your dominant foot.

Real-Life Science Challenge

How does being ambidextrous help in sports? In baseball, being a "switch hitter" can increase your chance of successfully hitting the baseball because you can choose which side to bat on based on which hand the pitcher is using to throw the ball.

In soccer, it is very difficult for a goalkeeper to try to guess to which side of the goal an ambidextrous kicker will kick the ball. It is also advantageous for the goalkeeper to be equally able to dive toward his or her left or right.

Fun Fact

While most people are "one-sided," meaning they have a dominant hand they use to do most things, and a few people are ambidextrous, meaning they can use both hands with equal ease, most animals are said to be ambidextrous. A few do have a right or left preference, such as lobsters and crabs, which are generally right-clawed, and rats, which are generally right-pawed.

Experiment

Now, start experimenting with testing for dominance of people's right or left feet.

Hints

☐ The people you test should not know what you are testing for.

☐ Have the same people do different types of tests and repeat each test several times.

☐ Remember that people usually start walking with their dominant foot.

Create an Optical Illusion

▓ What You Need to Know

An **optical illusion** is when something appears different from what it really is.

▓ How Do Optical Illusions Work?

What we see involves more than looking at something with our eyes. Sometimes, what we see is not what actually exists. The eyes send messages to the brain about the object viewed, and the brain interprets the message. An incorrect interpretation may cause you to "see" a misleading image, which is called an optical illusion.

▓ What Does This Have to Do with Creating Optical Illusions?

One type of optical illusion results from mistaking something due to the influence of background patterns. For example, look at the figure below. Which of the middle circles is larger, A or B?

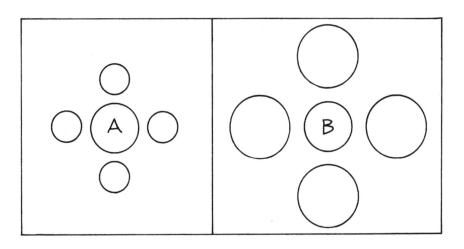

Circles A and B actually have the same diameter. However, what you *see* is that circle A, which is surrounded by small circles, looks larger than circle B, which is surrounded by large circles.

The figure below is another example of an optical illusion. Look at lines A and B in the figure. Are the lines curved or straight? Use a ruler to measure the distance between the lines at various points along the lines. The distance is the same, proving that lines A and B are actually straight and parallel. The radiating lines cause the image to appear as if the straight lines are curved.

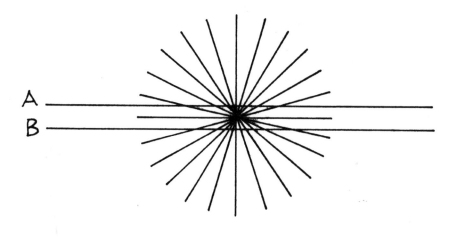

Real-Life Science Challenge

Why do you see things in three dimensions? The images seen by both your eyes overlap. This overlapped image is sent to the brain. It is the brain that interprets the message as being three-dimensional. This ability to recognize 3-D objects is called depth perception. Over time your brain stores information about how three-dimensional objects look, such as the shading on different sides of an object. While it takes two eyes to see in three dimensions, if you close one eye and look at a tree, or any other three-dimensional object, it still looks 3-D to you. This is because your brain is using stored information to interpret the message sent by your eye.

■ Experiment

Now, start experimenting with creating your own optical illusions.

Hints

☐ Angles and background shapes can change depth perception.

☐ Flipbooks are a type of optical illusion.

☐ Colors can be used to create a 3-D picture.

Fun Fact

In 1976, NASA launched the *Viking I* spacecraft with a mission of taking photos of the surface of Mars. These photos were to supply information for possible landing sites for a later spacecraft called *Viking II*. As *Viking I* orbited Mars taking photos, scientists watching in mission control were surprised when the shadowy likeness of a human face appeared to be looking back at them from Mars's surface. The shape was nearly two miles from end to end and located in a region called Cydonia. But the head turned out to be an optical illusion produced by the land features. Another optical illusion produced by shadows in Cydonia looks like an Egyptian pharaoh.

Clone a Plant

■ **What You Need to Know**

Cloning is the process of making an identical copy of an **organism** (a living thing). **Vegetative reproduction** is the cloning of a plant. **DNA** is the material inside the nucleus of every cell that contains the blueprint for all the characteristics of the organism.

■ **How Does Cloning Work?**

Every cell in your body contains DNA with the blueprint for your entire physical make up. For example, a heart cell contains DNA with all the information for eye color, hair color, height, whether you are a boy or girl, and so on. But during development, the DNA that develops into heart cells has the thousands of characteristics coded on it "silenced" except for heart characteristics. Nose cells have DNA with all characteristics silenced except for nose characteristics, and so on. In the process of cloning, scientists have found a way to give all the characteristics on the DNA in a single cell an active voice. This means that a new creature can develop from this single cell.

■ **What Does This Have to Do with Cloning Plants?**

In vegetative reproduction, the plant does not develop from a seed. Instead it develops from another part of the plant, such as the roots, the stems, or the leaves of a parent plant. The new plant is identical to the parent plant, so it is a clone. One method of using vegetative reproduction to grow new plants is the use of cuttings, also called **slips**. A cutting or slip is a piece of a stem or leaf that is capable of growing into a new plant. Cuttings grow into a new plant if a

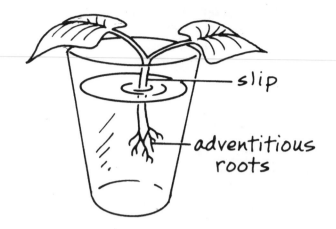

slip

adventitious roots

special type of root can grow at the end of the cutting. These roots are called **adventitious roots**. Some plants can be easily cloned from cuttings, while others can't.

Fun Fact

Is cloning a process that humans discovered? No. An example of natural cloning, or vegetative reproduction, is the strawberry plant. This plant grows **runners** (stems that grow across the surface of the ground). These runners develop roots, which grow into the ground, and new plants develop.

Real-Life Science Challenge

In 1952, the first animal, a tadpole, was cloned. The first **mammal** (any of a class of animals with backbones and that nurse their young), a sheep named Dolly, was cloned in 1997. Since Dolly's birth, other animals have been cloned.

Experiment

Now, start experimenting with vegetative reproduction.

Hints

☐ Research to find out which types of plants are easiest to clone.

☐ Think about what all plants need to grow.

☐ Take several cuttings from one kind of plant.

Determine if Seed Type Affects the Speed of Seed Growth

■ **What You Need to Know**

Germination is the process by which seeds begin to grow. The time it takes from planting a seed to the first signs of growth is called **germination starting time (GST)**. Seeds are one of the things that allow plants to **propagate** (produce new organisms). On the outside of a seed is a covering called a **seed coat**. Inside a seed is an **embryo**, which is an undeveloped plant in its earliest stages of development.

■ **How Does Germination Work?**

The embryo in a seed does not begin life when the seed starts germinating. Instead, the embryo resumes growth that stopped when the seed matured. Generally, the first visible sign of germination is the breaking of the seed coat. This allows nutrients that are not present in the seed, such as water and oxygen, to enter the seed so the embryo can develop.

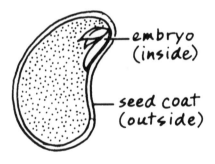

■ **What Does This Have to Do with the Speed of Seed Growth?**

One way to compare the growth speed of different seeds is to compare their germination starting time.

Corn and bean seeds have been found in Egyptian pyramids. These seeds germinated when they were planted. Because of the dry conditions where the seeds had been stored, they did not germinate but remained **dormant** (unproductive) for thousands of years.

Real-Life Science Challenge

Why are seeds being carried on spacecraft? By sending seeds on a shuttle mission or having them housed at the International Space Station (ISS) for an extended period, researchers can determine if, and how, the seeds are affected by the environmental conditions of space. This will help scientists to determine what types of seeds are more likely to germinate and grow in space, which is knowledge crucial to future long-term space missions.

■ Experiment

Now, start experimenting with seed germination.

Hints

☐ Keep all the variables, such as the amount of water, light, humidity, method of planting, and so on, the same for each type of planted seed.

☐ Create a way of germinating seeds so that you can observe changes daily.

Develop a Method for Determining a Plant's Rate of Transpiration

■ **What You Need to Know**

Vascular plants are plants that have special tubes for transporting **sap** (in plants, a watery solution with dissolved nutrients). The **xylem tubes** transport water and nutrients taken in through the roots throughout the plant. **Transpiration** is the release of water from a plant's surface. Most transpiration takes place in a plant's leaves. **Transpiration rate** is the measure of transpiration in a given time.

■ **How Does Transpiration Work?**

Transpiration is the process in which water is taken in by plant roots, moves up through xylem tubes, passes through holes in the leaves called **stomata**, and then evaporates into the atmosphere as water vapor. Sap moves through the xylem tubes in the stems, as shown in the diagram on page 49. As the water evaporates from the surface of the leaves, the column of sap in the xylem rises, and more water molecules are pulled in at the roots; thus, a continuous flow of water enters the roots and moves throughout the plant.

■ **What Does This Have to Do with Transpiration Rate?**

Plants control the amount of water lost by transpiration by opening and closing their stomata. Cells surrounding the stomata become more or less stiff, which causes the stomata to open or close. In a dry atmosphere, such as in a desert, the stomata of plants stay closed much of the time. This keeps the water inside the plant. Thus, desert plants have a low transpiration rate. The opposite is true of plants that grow in tropical rain forests.

Transpiration Process

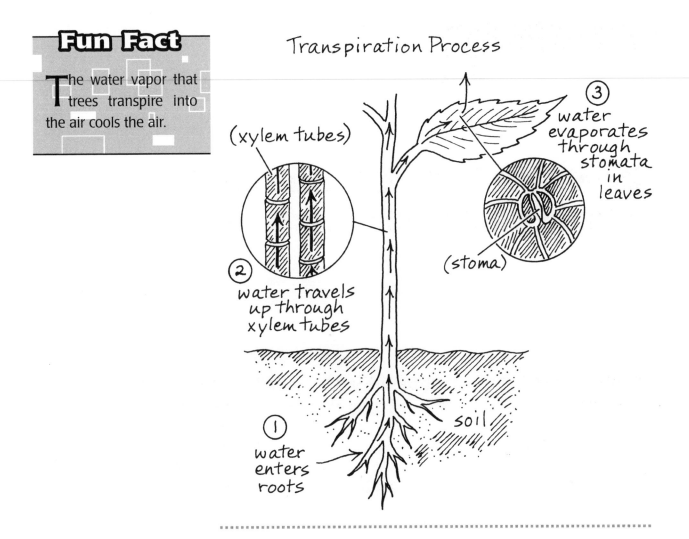

(xylem tubes)

② water travels up through xylem tubes

③ water evaporates through stomata in leaves

(stoma)

① water enters roots

soil

Real-Life Science Challenge

Plant transpiration rate is affected by **humidity** (the measure of the amount of moisture in the air). If the humidity is too high, the transpiration rate will be so low that the plant cannot pass the oxygen and water it produces back into the atmosphere. When this happens, the plant's growth can be stunted or the plant may even die. This can happen in greenhouses that don't have proper ventilation or if plants are watered too much.

■ Experiment

Now, start experimenting with transpiration rate.

Hints

☐ Decide on a way to measure how much water the plant gives off.

☐ Think about how to collect the water that is given off by a plant's leaves in a specific amount of time.

Show That Fruits Contain Germination Inhibitors

What You Need to Know

In reference to plants, an **inhibitor** is a chemical that blocks plant growth. A **germination inhibitor** is a chemical that prevents the germination of seeds.

How Does a Germination Inhibitor Work?

Plants can produce their own germination inhibitors. The germination inhibitor produced by a plant prevents the germination of its own seeds until conditions are favorable for them to develop. Common substances that seem to reduce seed germination include tomato juice, lemon peel, onion juice, apple cider, and the water in which carrots or spinach have been cooked.

What Does This Have to Do with Fruits?

Most fruits contain germination inhibitors, which prevent the seeds from germinating while they are inside the fruit. When the fruit falls to the ground, and its fleshy part decays, water washing over the soil will wash the inhibitor off the seed. The seed from the fruit can then grow.

Inhibitors in one plant can prevent the growth of another plant. Some plants, such as sweet potatoes, release special chemicals called **allelochemicals** that prevent other plants from growing too close to them. Organic gardeners use plants that contain allelochemicals to keep weeds away from crops, and scientists are looking for ways to use allelochemicals as natural weed killers.

Fun Fact

When animals, such as birds and bats, swallow seeds, the germination inhibitors are removed as the seeds pass through the digestive system of the animal. When these seeds are eliminated from the body along with the animal's feces, they are ready to germinate.

■ Experiment

Now, start experimenting with ways to show that different fruits contain germination inhibitors.

Hints

☐ The germination inhibitor might be in the seed coat or it might be in the flesh of the fruit.

☐ Try making extracts of different fruits and different fruit parts.

☐ Determine the effect of the fruit extracts on the germination of seeds.

Determine if the Head of a Sunflower Is Made of Complete or Incomplete Flowers

■ **What You Need to Know**

A **complete flower** is one that has sepals, petals, stamens, and pistils. The **pistil** is the female part of a flower and the **stamen** is the male part. **Petals** are leaflike structures, often brightly colored, which surround and protect the pistil and stamen. **Sepals** are leaflike structures, usually green, that surround and protect the flower before it opens. An **incomplete flower** is one that lacks one of the four basic flower parts. A special petallike leaf is called a **bract**. A **composite flower** is made of many separate flowers that together are called a **head**.

■ **How Do Composite Flowers Work?**

Composite flowers are one of the largest groups of flowering plants. Each composite flower, such as the sunflower, the daisy, the goldenrod, and the dandelion, looks like a single flower, but each one is really many separate flowers grouped together into the flower head. The head of many composite flowers is made of two kinds of flowers. In the center of the head are **disk flowers**, and around the disk flowers are the **ray flowers**, which often look like petals. The heads of some composite flowers, such as dandelions, are made of groups of ray flowers only, and some are groups of disk flowers only.

■ **What Does This Have to Do with a Flower Being Incomplete or Complete?**

A complete flower, such as a rose, has the four parts: sepals, petals, stamens, and a pistil. The poinsettia, on the other hand, is an incomplete flower because it lacks petals. What look like bright red petals are actually bracts. The dogwood is a special flower. What look like

Composite Flower

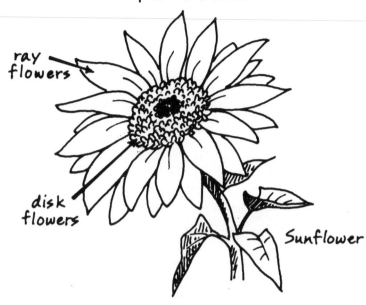

ray flowers

disk flowers

Sunflower

white leaves are bracts, but the flower is complete because each flower has its own tiny petals, sepals, stamens, and pistil.

Real-Life Science Challenge

Poinsettias are popular flowers that are sold during the Christmas season. People who grow these plants need them to bloom at a certain time of the year. Scientists have helped solve this problem by studying what makes a flower bloom. One of the main factors influencing when a flower blooms is the length of time it is exposed to daylight. Poinsettias are **short day plants**, meaning they require short periods of daylight and long periods of night in order to prepare for flowering. If the plants are kept in greenhouses where the lights are on for part of the night, the plants' natural blooming schedule is delayed. When growers are ready for the plants to bloom, they turn off the lights, and the plants bloom naturally.

Now, start experimenting with ways to study the different flowers that make up the head of a sunflower.

Hints

☐ Create a way to separate the flowers in the head of the sunflower without destroying their structure.

☐ Try using a magnifying lens to identify the parts of the separate flowers.

Determine the Rate of Geotropism of Plant Stems

What You Need to Know

Tropism is the growth of plants in response to **stimuli**, which are things that an organism responds to. If the stimulus is gravity, the response is called **geotropism**. Plant growth in the direction of the force of gravity, toward the center of Earth, is called **positive geotropism**. Plant growth in the opposite direction of the force of gravity is called **negative geotropism**. **Auxin** is a chemical in plants that affects plant growth.

How Does Geotropism Work?

If a plant were lying on its side, gravity would cause a buildup of auxin on the lower part of the plant's stems and roots. This high concentration of auxin causes plant stem cells to grow faster. Thus, the lower part of the stem would have longer cells, which would result in the stem bending upward as shown in the figure on page 56. Plant stem cell growth represents negative geotropism. Root cells have an opposite response to auxin. This represents positive geotropism. A high concentration of auxin causes root cells to grow more slowly. So the cells in the upper part of the root grow longer, resulting in the root bending down.

What Does This Have to Do with the Rate of Geotropism?

The **rate of geotropism**, or **gravitropism**, is a measure of the time it takes a plant stem or root to respond to gravity.

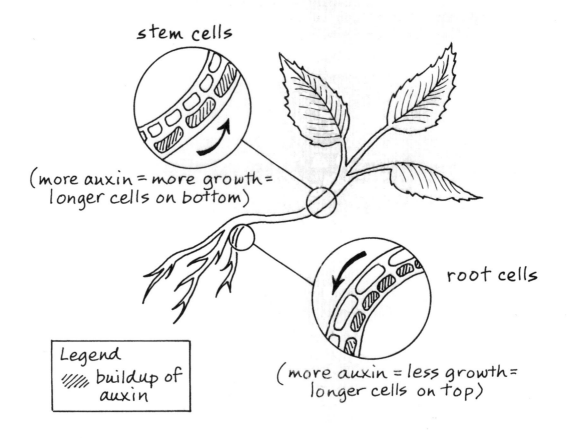

stem cells

(more auxin = more growth = longer cells on bottom)

root cells

(more auxin = less growth = longer cells on top)

Legend
///// buildup of auxin

Real-Life Science Challenge

Prolonged spaceflights will require the growth of plants for water purification, atmospheric conditioning, nutrient recycling, and food production. In environments with zero or reduced gravity, the stems and roots of plants grow in random directions. Scientists are still investigating how to solve this problem. What solutions do you suggest?

■ **Experiment**

Now, start experimenting with plants and rates of geotropism.

Hints

☐ Obtain a few samples of one kind of plant.

☐ Plant plants at different angles.

☐ Determine a method for measuring geotropism over time.

CHALLENGE

20

BIOLOGY

Determine the Effect of Gray Water on Plant Growth

■ **What You Need to Know**

Gray water is used household water that does not include **sewage** (toilet water), otherwise known as **black water**. Gray water is **nonpotable**, meaning that it is not fit for drinking.

■ **How Does Gray Water Work?**

Gray water is used household water, such as from sinks, bathtubs, showers, and washing machines. In some dry climates, houses have plumbing that allows the gray water to be reused as shown in the figure on page 58. Pipes carrying gray water are labeled so it is clear that the water is nonpotable.

■ **What Does This Have to Do with Plant Growth?**

Water is necessary for plant growth. Some people use gray water to water plants. Gray water often has different kinds of soap (washing soap, hand soap, bath soap, shampoo, etc.) in it. Do these solutes affect plant growth?

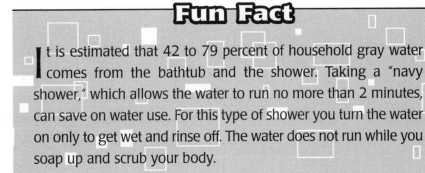

Fun Fact

It is estimated that 42 to 79 percent of household gray water comes from the bathtub and the shower. Taking a "navy shower," which allows the water to run no more than 2 minutes, can save on water use. For this type of shower you turn the water on only to get wet and rinse off. The water does not run while you soap up and scrub your body.

gray water

plants

Real-Life Science Challenge

Is it safe to use gray water on plants? Kitchen gray water should not be reused because the food particles in the water decay. The bacteria causing the decay could affect the plants' growth. Gray water from the washing machine should not be reused if it is contaminated by soiled diapers or clothes, materials used by people with infectious diseases, or materials used in poultry or wild game preparation. The health risks from gray water are considered minimal if you handle and apply it properly. Six basic precautions when using gray water are:

1. Use it the same day it's collected.
2. Don't apply it where people will come in contact with it, such as on a lawn.
3. Don't use it to water food crops.
4. Don't let it puddle or stand. (Make sure it is absorbed quickly.)
5. Don't spray it or sprinkle it in any way. Instead, pour it.
6. Whenever you handle gray water or equipment that's in contact with it, wear rubber gloves.

■ Experiment

Now, start experimenting with how gray water affects plant growth.

Hints

☐ Determine the best way to collect gray water.

☐ Use different sources of gray water to determine its different effects.

☐ Use the same type of plant.

☐ Control variables like the amount of water, the method of watering, and so on.

PART III

Chemistry Challenges

Keep Iron from Rusting

■ **What You Need to Know**

A **chemical reaction** is the change in the arrangement of particles in one or more substances called **reactants**, resulting in the formation of one or more new substances called **products**. **Corrosion** is the slow eating away of a metal due to a chemical reaction. **Rusting** is a common name for the corrosion of iron in the presence of water and oxygen. **Rust** is the reddish iron oxide formed by the rusting process.

■ **How Does a Chemical Reaction Work?**

In a chemical reaction, the particles making up the reactants break apart and rearrange themselves in a different way. Take a look at the gumdrop-shaped models of chemicals shown in the diagram below. Notice that the same number of each kind of gumdrop in the reactants make up the products. They've just become linked together in a different way.

Chemical Reaction

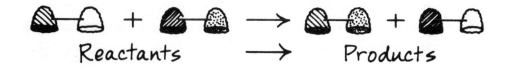

Reactants → Products

What Does This Have to Do with Rusting Iron?

Rusting is a chemical reaction. The reactants are iron and oxygen and the product is iron oxide (rust). For rusting to occur, the iron atoms must lose some of their **electrons** (negative particles that travel around the nucleus of an atom), and the oxygen must gain them. Water is needed for rusting to occur because the electrons that the iron loses travel through the water. The chemical reaction expressed in words for the rusting of iron is:

iron + oxygen *yields* iron oxide

Real-Life Science Challenge

Steel is a mixture of iron and carbon. One way that scientists have discovered to keep iron in steel from rusting is to **galvanize** it, which means to coat it with zinc. Zinc is rust-resistant.

Experiment

Now, start experimenting with iron. How can you prevent it from rusting?

Hints

☐ Use small iron pieces of equal size, such as ungalvanized steel nails.

☐ Experiment with different ways of coating the iron pieces, such as with oil, paint, or nail polish.

Fun Fact

The *Titanic* is sitting on the ocean bottom at a depth where there is little to no oxygen. Yet iron in the ship is corroding. One evidence of this corrosion are structures, called **rusticles**, that are huge, rust-colored, iciclelike masses of rust. Instead of oxygen in the water causing this rust, it is created by iron-eating bacteria that have been feasting on the *Titanic's* iron. The chemical reactions during the bacteria's digestive processes produce the waste that forms the rusticles. Despite their size, the rusticle structures are very fragile and burst into clouds of red dust if they are even lightly touched. Little by little the *Titanic* is being eaten away. Eventually, it will be a pile of red rust. Some say this may happen in less than 100 years. In the meantime, scientists are working to determine how the bacteria are making this chemical change.

Determine How the Rate of Diffusion of a Material Is Affected by the Shape of the Container It's In

■ What You Need to Know

Diffusion is the movement of particles from one place to another. The **rate of diffusion** is the time it takes for particles to separate and spread evenly, forming a **homogeneous mixture** (a mixture that is the same throughout).

■ How Does Diffusion Work?

Diffusion is the spreading out of particles from a concentrated area. Diffusion occurs because the random movement of particles allows them to separate from one another. Two things that influence diffusion are the space between particles and the speed of the particles. The greater the space between particles and the greater their speed, the greater their ability to spread out from one another. The more packed the particles are in a substance, the more difficult it is for them to move, thus the more difficult it is for diffusion to occur. For example, solid substances are made of particles that are tightly packed together, so they diffuse very slowly. If you stacked a lead brick on top of a gold brick and left them undisturbed for several years, some of the gold atoms would diffuse into the lead brick and some of the lead atoms would diffuse into the gold brick, but most of the material would remain unchanged. On the other hand, the particles of liquids are less packed, move faster, and diffuse more quickly. For example, one drop of food coloring in a glass of water will noticeably diffuse throughout the water in minutes, or hours depending on the amount of water. The particles of a gas are much more distant from one another and move faster than either liquid or solid particles. It takes only a short time for gas particles to diffuse.

In fact, if the gas cannot be seen but has an odor, it is only the smell that indicates that the gas particles have spread. When a skunk sprays its musk, at first only animals and people near the skunk can smell it. In a short time, the odor can be smelled at great distances from the skunk.

■ **What Does This Have to Do with How the Shape of a Container Affects Diffusion Rate?**

Diffusion is the result of the motion of particles. Because of **inertia** (the property of all objects that resists a change in motion or direction), things in motion continue in the same direction unless some force stops them or changes their direction. When particles diffuse, their direction is changed when they bounce into one another, when they bounce into the particles of the substance they are diffusing through, and when they bounce into the sides of the container they are in. In a narrow container, particles diffuse faster because they bounce back and forth from the sides more often than in a wide container.

■ Experiment

Now, start experimenting with how the shape of a container affects the speed of diffusion.

Hints

☐ Find containers that are different shapes but about the same size.

☐ Diffusion of a colored solute in a colorless solvent is easy to see, and its movements are easy to measure.

☐ Use the same kind and amount of diffusing material (solute) and the same kind of solvent for each test.

Fun Fact

On Earth, gravity influences the diffusion rate of particles. In molten metals, temperature differences cause the warmer, less dense particles to rise and the colder, more dense atoms to fall. This movement of particles affects the diffusion process. In space, scientists have the opportunity to study diffusion in liquid metals without the effects of gravity. Therefore, they can determine the true diffusion rate in different liquid metals. This information could ultimately lead to better automotive, airplane, and building materials.

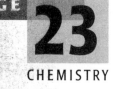
Determine Which Type of Polymer Food Wrap Is Best at Preventing Food Dehydration

■ What You Need to Know

Polymers are long molecules made up of repeating units linked together by chemical bonds. **Dehydration** is excessive loss of water. **Permeability** is the ability of a material to allow a substance to pass through it without affecting the material. **Evaporation** is the change of the molecules on the surface of a liquid to a gas.

■ How Does a Polymer Work?

Polymers are substances whose molecules are made of large numbers of repeating units, much like a train with many cars attached. Proteins and starches such as silk and **cellulose** (the tough material in plant stems) are examples of natural polymers. Plastics are an example of **synthetic** (man-made) polymers. Synthetic polymers are formed by chemical reactions in which many separate units are joined into a chain. There are three different kinds of polymers used for kitchen plastic wrap: polyethylene (such as Glad or Handi-wrap); polyvinyl chloride (such as Reynolds Wrap); and polyvinylidene chloride (such as Saran Premium Wrap).

■ What Does This Have to Do with Food Dehydration?

Water in food evaporates. If the food is covered with plastic food wrap, the water vapor collects in the space between the food and the plastic wrap. If the plastic wrap is permeable to water vapor, the water vapor escapes through the wrap, and the food can become dehydrated. The amount of water that escapes depends on how permeable the plastic is. In the diagram on page 69, there is more

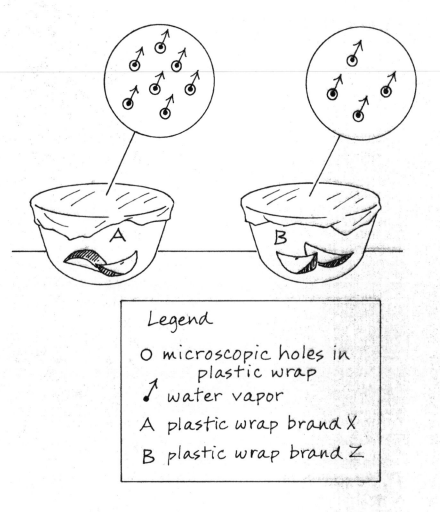

Legend

O microscopic holes in plastic wrap

↗ water vapor

A plastic wrap brand X

B plastic wrap brand Z

water leaving through the plastic wrap covering bowl A than there is through the wrap covering bowl B. The food in bowl A will dehydrate faster than the food in bowl B.

Real-Life Science Challenge

To limit permeability to moisture, films of polycarbonate, polyester, or polyethylene plastics are sometimes laminated together. Some also have metallic layers. Military food, packaged in such metallized plastic wrap, has a very long shelf life (five years or longer) if kept cool.

■ **Experiment**

Now, start experimenting with different kinds of plastic food wraps, and determine how good they are at preventing food dehydration.

Hints

☐ Before testing the wraps on actual food, design an experiment to test each type of wrap's permeability to water vapor.

☐ Design a method for determining the rate of evaporation.

☐ Using containers of water instead of food will make measuring evaporation easier.

Fun Fact

A helium balloon is actually filled with a mixture of helium gas and air. The balloon is permeable to helium but not to air. This is because the molecules that make up air are bigger than the holes in the rubber balloon, but the molecules of helium gas are smaller than the holes. Over time, usually one day, the helium will pass through the small holes in the balloon, leaving the larger particles of air behind. When the helium leaks out, the balloon is partially inflated because of the air in it, but it does not float.

Many inventions by NASA for its space missions are also part of our everyday lives. One such material (used by NASA to insulate and protect astronauts and their instruments) is now used to make the foil balloons that are filled with a mixture of air and helium. Foil balloons are made from a sheet of nylon coated on one side with polyethylene and a thin coating of metal on the other side. Unlike latex balloons, commonly called rubber balloons, the surfaces of foil balloons have smaller spaces, which keep the helium gas inside for a much longer time.

Determine the Effect of Temperature on the Adhesion of Polyvinyl Acetate Glue

■ **What You Need to Know**

Polyvinyl acetate is a type of polymer called **thermoplastic**, which means it can be melted and reformed over and over. **Adhesion** is the bonding force between unlike particles.

■ **How Does Adhesion Work?**

Adhesion occurs when two different kinds of molecules link together. An adhesive, such as liquid white glue, is basically a mixture of the polymer "polyvinyl acetate" and water. When applied between two surfaces, the water in the glue evaporates and the polyvinyl acetate molecules bond to one another and to the surfaces the glue touches.

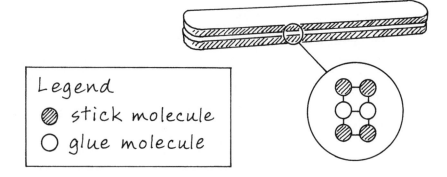

Legend
⊘ stick molecule
○ glue molecule

What Does This Have to Do with How Temperatures Affect Adhesion of Polyvinyl Acetate Glue?

When polyvinyl acetate is dry, it is a leathery, colorless, thermoplastic material. This type of glue works best in a narrow temperature range of 65°F (18°C) to 72°F (22°C). But what happens to the adhesive properties of dried glue if it is frozen?

Fun Fact

The polymer **casein**, which comes from milk, is used in adhesives, paints, and even plastics. You can make casein glue by mixing 1 tablespoon (15 mL) of vinegar with 7 tablespoons (105 mL) of nonfat or skim milk. The white clumps that form are called curds, and the liquid is called whey. The curds are made of the polymer casein. Separate the curds and the whey and the curds can be used to glue paper together. How well does your homemade glue work compared to other glues?

Real-Life Science Challenge

Inventors are being challenged to create an adhesive that can be activated by human body fluids, such as blood or saliva, or by an outside source, such as light or radiation. The ideal adhesive would hold tissues together long enough for them to grow together, then lose its strength and be absorbed by the body.

Experiment

Now, start experimenting with how different temperatures affect the adhesive properties of polyvinyl acetate glue.

Hints

☐ Design a way to measure how adhesive the glue is.

☐ Test one brand of glue on different types of surfaces.

☐ Any white school glue can be used.

☐ Try using a refrigerator and a freezer to lower the glue's temperature.

Make Recycled Paper

■ **What You Need to Know**

Fiber is a hairlike strand of material that is much longer than it is wide. **Plant fiber** is made of dead plant cells that are long, narrow, and **tapered** (gradually narrower toward the end) at each end. **Fiber cells** are made mostly of the chemicals cellulose and lignin. **Paper** is a thin sheet made from **pulp**, which is a mixture of water and separated plant fibers. **Recycle** means to process a material so it can be used again.

■ **How Does Papermaking Work?**

Plant fibers are threadlike strands of dead cells that are characterized by an elongated shape and a thick cell wall composed mainly of cellulose and lignin. In plant fibers, such as wood, the tapered ends of the cells overlap. The length of the fiber depends on the number of cells that make it up. Fiber length varies from one type of plant to another. Wood fiber used for papermaking is generally about $\frac{1}{10}$ inch to $\frac{1}{4}$ inch (2.54 mm to 6.35 mm) in length. Mixing short and long fibers increases paper strength.

Most paper is made with wood fibers. After grinding and treating the fiber with various chemicals, only cellulose is left in it. This fiber plus water is called pulp. Next, the pulp goes through a process to separate the individual wood fibers. The mushy pulp mixture is sprayed onto a long, wide screen, called a wire. Water starts to drain out of the holes in the wire. This water is collected and recycled to make more pulp. As the water drains, the wood fibers begin to stick together, forming a very thin mat on the wire. Felt-covered rollers are used to absorb more of the water. But the pulpy mat on the wire

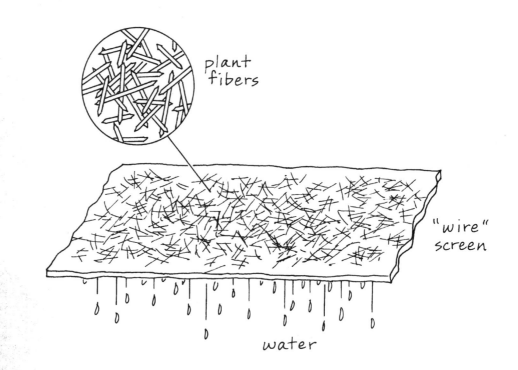

plant fibers

"wire" screen

water

is still about 60 percent water. The wire is now passed through hot rollers. The rollers heat and dry the wet mat, sealing the fibers closer and closer together, gradually changing them from pulp to paper. A big heavy roller presses the dry paper to make it smooth and uniform in thickness. The paper might then be coated with a fine layer of clay to make it glossier and easier to print on. After some more drying, the paper-making process is complete.

■ What Does This Have to Do with Recycling Paper?

In recycling, pulp is made by mixing wastepaper with water. Wastepaper that has never been used is called mill broke. If recycled paper contains more than 25 percent mill broke pulp, it is not considered recycled. Wastepaper that has print on it is called post-consumer waste. It is more difficult to recycle this type of paper because the ink has to be removed during the recycling process.

Fun Fact

Some insects, such as paper wasps and yellow jackets, make paper nests. They mix their saliva with fibers scraped from dead wood until a pulp similar to papier-mâché is formed. The nests contain a single layer of six-sided chambers that fit neatly together, like the cells of a honeycomb. *Caution:* Don't ever disturb a wasp's or a bee's nest. Wasps and bees are easily provoked and can sting forcibly, causing much pain, as this author can testify.

Paper makes up a large percentage of the waste in landfills in the United States. Recycling paper is one way to reduce the amount of trash in landfills. Recycled paper also helps save energy and water because most of the energy and water in papermaking is used to change wood into pulp. Paper can be recycled only 4 to 6 times. This is because with each recycling, the fibers get shorter and weaker. New pulp must be mixed with the recycled fibers to maintain the strength and quality of the paper.

■ Experiment

Now, start experimenting with papermaking. Which paper is easiest to recycle? Which makes the best recycled paper? What about a mixture of different kinds of papers?

Hints

☐ Research the history of papermaking.

☐ Collect scraps of different types of paper.

☐ Make pulp by mixing water with bits of wastepaper.

☐ How can you safely remove the ink from used paper?

☐ How will you dry your paper?

Find the Most Absorbent Brand of Paper Towels

What You Need to Know

Absorb means to soak up. **Porous** means to have many small holes. **Capillary action** is the movement of a liquid, such as water, through a very small space due to adhesion and surface tension. **Surface tension** is the attraction between molecules at the surface of a liquid. This attraction is due to **cohesion**, which is the bonding force between like particles.

How Does Capillary Action Work?

Capillary action occurs when a liquid, such as water, is in a narrow vessel. Adhesion of water molecules to the walls of the vessel causes an upward force on the liquid at the edges and results in these molecules moving up the walls. The surface tension, which acts much like a skin across the water's surface, holds the water molecules together. So instead of just the edges of the water moving upward, the whole liquid surface is dragged upward, creating a curved surface as shown in the diagram.

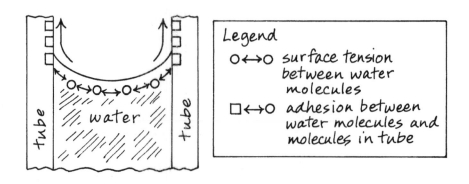

Cotton can absorb up to 27 times its own weight in water. This is why bath towels are generally made of cotton. The most absorbent towels are made with looped strands of cotton on both sides of the towel because the loops act like very small sponges. Loosely twisted loops are softer and more absorbent than tightly twisted loops, which produce a rougher fabric.

The height to which capillary action will lift water depends on the weight of water that the surface tension can lift. As shown in the diagram below, the narrower the tube the higher capillary action can lift the water.

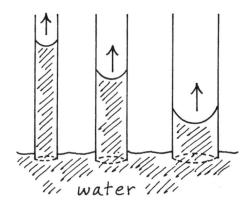

water

What Does This Have to Do with Paper Towel Absorbency?

The fibers in paper towels are surrounded by different-sized spaces that are interconnected. The spaces between the fibers are small enough that the effects of capillary action can take place when the paper towel is placed on a liquid. The more narrow the space between the fibers the farther the liquid moves.

Real-Life Science Challenge

Disposable paper diapers absorb better now because of NASA. This is because extra-absorbent diapers were needed for astronauts. It was discovered that adding sodium polyacrylate to the paper fibers in a diaper produced a safe superabsorbent diaper.

Experiment

Now, start experimenting with the absorbency of different kinds of paper towels.

Hints

- ☐ Cut paper towels into equal-size strips.
- ☐ Make a testing apparatus to dip the strips in equal amounts of water.
- ☐ Determine how to measure the absorbency of the paper.

Separate the Substances in a Mixture

What You Need to Know

A **mixture** is a combination of two or more substances that can be separated by physical means. A solid that will dissolve in a liquid is said to be **soluble** in that liquid. A solid that will not dissolve in a liquid is **insoluble** in that liquid. **Filtration** is the physical process of using a porous substance (a **filter**) to separate a solid from a liquid. The liquid that passes through the filter is called the **filtrate**, and the solid collected by the filter is called the **residue**.

How Does a Mixture Work?

A mixture contains substances that retain their separate identities. The individual substances remain visible in some mixtures, such as a mixture of salt and pepper. In other mixtures, the dissolving substance breaks into particles that are too small to see. For example, a mixture of sugar and water forms a solution in which the sugar particles are present but are not visible.

What Does This Have to Do with Separating Substances in a Mixture?

The process of separating particles in a mixture depends on the characteristics of the particles. For example, an insoluble solid, such as a rock mixed with water, can be separated by filtration. Soluble substances must be separated by other methods. For example, a mixture of sugar and water forms a solution in which the sugar particles can be separated by evaporation of the water.

sugar + water ⟹ sugar + water solution

Real-Life Science Challenge

Pollutants (any unwanted substance) that are spilled into the ocean have to be separated and taken out of the water to protect marine life. The characteristics of the pollutants determine what processes are used for this separation. Oil spills are very damaging to wild-life. For example, oil on the wings of birds makes it difficult or impossible for the birds to fly. Much of the spilled oil can be separated from the water because oil is insoluble in water. It is also less dense than water, which causes it to float on the surface of the water. This makes it possible to remove the oil by sucking it off the surface. Unfortunately, spilled oil that reaches the shore covers rocks and is absorbed by the sand. This oil can kill things living in these areas and is difficult to remove.

Perfume is a solution of a solvent and different solutes. The solutes include the scents called "**notes**." Just as musical notes must be combined to create music, scent notes are combined to make certain fragrances. The scent notes separate from the mixture as they evaporate at different rates. The notes that evaporate first are called the top notes. These are light fragrances that you smell when you first open a perfume bottle, and they last a few minutes. The middle notes are apparent about 15 minutes after application and last about one hour. The bottom notes are the last to evaporate, and their fragrance lasts the longest, usually several hours.

Now, start experimenting with separating the particles in different kinds of mixtures.

Caution: You want to mix substances that do not create chemical reactions. Have an adult supervise and approve the mixtures you make. Avoid household cleansers, which can produce toxic materials when mixed together.

Hints

☐ Safe substances to mix include water, tempera paints, food coloring, fruit juices, salt, sugar, pepper, Epsom salts, and dirt.

☐ Physical characteristics of substances can sometimes lead to unique separation techniques. For example, magnets can be used to separate magnetic materials from nonmagnetic ones.

☐ Filters can be porous papers, such as a coffee filter, or a porous solid, such as charcoal or sand.

Make More of a Solute Dissolve in Water

■ **What You Need to Know**

When no more solute can dissolve in a solvent, the solution is said to be a **saturated solution**. If the solvent is water, the solution is called an **aqueous solution**. A **supersaturated solution** means that it has more solute than is normally possible at a certain temperature. Syrup is a supersaturated sugar solution, as is honey.

■ **How Does a Saturated Solution Work?**

Generally, the solvent of a solution makes up the largest part of the solution, and the solute, which makes up the smallest part, breaks down to its smallest particles and spreads evenly throughout the solvent. An aqueous solution is a mixture of water and another substance, which can be a gas, a liquid, or a solid. Only a certain amount of a solute can dissolve in a solvent. For example, some of the air blown into the water of an aquarium dissolves, but most of it forms bubbles and rises to the surface where it escapes. This is because the water becomes saturated with air and no more can dissolve.

aerator

What Does This Have to Do with Making More Solute Dissolve in Water?

Before determining how to increase the amount of solute, the type of solute has to be identified. If the solute is a gas, an increase in pressure increases the amount of gas that dissolves. For example, more carbon dioxide gas is dissolved in water under pressure in carbonated drinks. When the pressure is released by opening the bottle or can, the carbon dioxide gas quickly separates from the water in the form of bubbles. However, pressure has little to no effect on the amount of liquids or solids that can dissolve in water. An increase in temperature makes some liquids and solids more soluble and others less soluble. How does a temperature change affect the amount of common solutes, such as sugar and salt, that dissolve in water?

Fun Fact

Packaged hand warmers are made with supersaturated solutions. Bending the package causes the excess solute to **crystallize** (particles bond together, forming a solid). The process of crystallization is a type of chemical reaction that gives off heat causing the temperature of the package to rise to about 130° F for about 30 minutes.

Real-Life Science Challenge

Artificial sweeteners can help a person cut down on calories and help manage diabetes, a health condition that results from an abnormal amount of blood sugar. Aspartame is a common artificial sweetener that has the same amount of calories as an equal amount of sugar. The difference is that aspartame is 180 times sweeter than sugar, so only a small amount has to be used to make a solution as sweet as sugar. Even though the solubility of aspartame decreases with temperature, enough can be dissolved in an icy drink to make it sweet. Could enough sugar be dissolved at the same temperature to make the drink as sweet?

Experiment

Now, start experimenting with making more of a solute dissolve in water.

Hints

☐ Solutes might include sugar, salt, Epsom salts, or artificial sweeteners.

☐ Ask for adult assistance if you use hot water.

☐ Carefully measure how much of the solvent you add to the water.

☐ When the water is saturated with the solute, the excess solute will not dissolve.

Design Ways to Test Water Hardness

■ **What You Need to Know**

Hard water contains high levels of minerals, mostly calcium and magnesium. **Soft water** contains little or no calcium and/or magnesium.

■ **How Does Hard Water Work?**

Hard or soft water is not a comparison of how firm the water is to the touch. Instead it is a comparison of how hard it is to make soap suds in the water. The calcium and magnesium particles in hard water react with soap and form a substance that does not make suds. The higher the levels are of these minerals in water, the harder the water and the more soap it takes to make suds. In the diagrams below and on page 84, the same amount of bubble bath has been added to both baths. The tub filled with hard water has few bubbles, and the one with soft water has many.

Fun Fact

The ring that forms in your bathtub after draining the water from a bath is due to the hardness of your water. The harder the water is, the bigger the ring will be. The minerals in the water react with the bath soap to form an insoluble substance known as soap scum. Soap scum does not easily wash away.

soft water

hard water

What Does This Have to Do with Testing Water Hardness?

Testing kits can be used for determining water hardness, but simple home tests can be designed to measure the relative hardness of water.

Real-Life Science Challenge

Clothes that are washed in hard water may appear dingy compared to those washed in soft water. This is because the minerals in hard water combine with parts of the dirt and oils on the clothes and form insoluble substances that are difficult to remove. Continuous washing in hard water can damage cloth fibers and shorten the life of clothes. Water softening devices can be used to remove the water-hardening minerals from the water in your home.

Experiment

Now, start experimenting with different ways to test for water hardness.

Hints

☐ Distilled water, which has no minerals in it, can be used as a control.

☐ Mixing distilled water with Epsom salts, which contain magnesium, can make samples of water of different hardnesses.

☐ Liquid soap can be measured in small amounts, such as by drops.

Find Out Which Color Pigments Are Hidden in a Green Leaf

■ **What You Need to Know**

Chromatography is a procedure for separating the parts of a solution by the use of an absorbing material. **Pigment** is a substance that gives color.

■ **How Does Chromatography Work?**

Color pigments in a solution can be separated by chromatography. One method of separating these pigments is to make a mark on a strip of filter paper with a colored solution. Allow the paper to dry, then hang the strip of paper in a solvent such as water. As the paper absorbs the solvent, it slowly moves up the paper, and the dry solute on the paper dissolves in the solvent. The solute is made of different pigments, which have different characteristics, including attraction to the paper. These differences result in the pigments moving different distances through the paper. The diagram shows a mark containing pigments from a mixture of blue, red, and yellow food coloring. As the water moves through the paper, the pigments separate in this order: blues separate first, followed by yellow, and finally red.

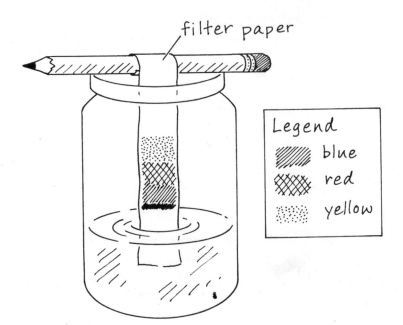

filter paper

Legend
///// blue
XXXX red
····· yellow

Green leaves get their color from **chlorophyll** (a green pigment found in plants), but green isn't the only color hidden in the leaves. Think about the colors leaves turn in the fall.

Real-Life Science Challenge

Chromatography is used today in some industries to separate and identify chemicals. It is also used in **forensic science** (the use of science to investigate physical evidence used in a court of law). For example, amounts of poisons and drugs, including narcotics and even aspirin, can be detected by paper chromatography in urine or blood samples. It can also be used to test athletes for performance-enhancing drugs like steroids.

Experiment

Now, start experimenting to see what colors you can find in different green leaves.

Hints

☐ Coffee filters are good chromatography papers.

☐ Determine different methods of extracting the green color from a leaf, such as dissolving it in a solvent.

PART IV

Earth Science Challenges

Determine How the Physical Characteristics of Earth's Surface Affect Climate

■ **What You Need to Know**

The **atmosphere** is the layer of air surrounding Earth. **Air** is a mixture of gases in Earth's atmosphere. **Weather** is atmospheric conditions over a short time, such as air temperature and humidity. **Climate** is the average weather in a region over a long period of time. **Energy** is the ability to cause something to move or change. **Radiation** is a type of energy that travels in waves, without physical substance. **Solar energy** is radiation energy from the Sun. The Sun emits different types of radiation, such as **visible radiation** (the light you can see) and **infrared radiation** (heat energy you can't see). The **greenhouse effect** is the heating that occurs when gases in the atmosphere allow sunlight to pass through to Earth's surface but trap infrared radiation leaving from Earth's surface.

■ **How Does the Greenhouse Effect Work?**

Earth's atmosphere acts as an insulator. This means it is like a blanket that helps keep Earth's heat from escaping into space. This blanket of air allows sunlight to pass through to Earth. Some of the sunlight that hits Earth's surface is reflected back into space. The sunlight that is absorbed by surface materials causes the materials to increase in temperature. The warm surface gives off heat in the form of infrared radiation. Gases in the atmosphere absorb this heat. In turn, the heated gas particles also give off infrared radiation, some of which is sent back to Earth. This back-and-forth heat transfer is called the greenhouse effect, and the gases that absorb the heat, mainly carbon dioxide and water vapor, are called greenhouse gases.

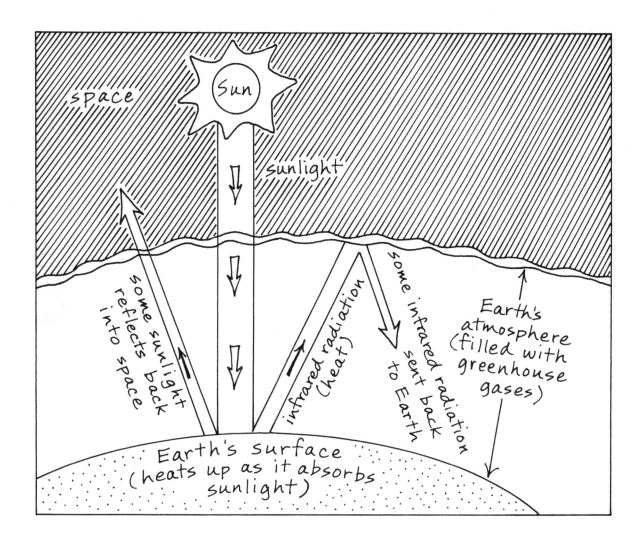

What Does This Have to Do with Surface Characteristics Affecting Earth's Climate?

The greenhouse effect is responsible for the temperature of Earth and of the lower atmosphere. The amount of heating and cooling is influenced by different factors, but the physical characteristics of Earth's surface are the most important. This is because how the surface absorbs, reflects, and radiates radiation determines how much heat is produced. For example, sunlight falling on a white,

Fun Fact

In a desert, where there is very little water vapor in the atmosphere, the nighttime temperature can be as much as 80° F (26° C) lower than daytime temperatures. Without the protection of the atmosphere, some places on Earth would be about 176° F (80° C) during the day and −220° F (−140° C) at night.

slick glacier surface is strongly reflected back into space, resulting in minimal heating of the surface and the lower atmosphere. On the other hand, sunlight falling on dark, rough desert soil is strongly absorbed and results in significant heating of the surface and the lower atmosphere.

Real-Life Science Challenge

Life on Earth could not survive without the greenhouse effect. But is the increased production of greenhouse gases from the burning of fossil fuels causing global warming? Some say it is, but others say it isn't. The problem is that records of the weather have not been thoroughly kept for a long enough period of time to determine if there really is **global warming**, which would be a permanent warming change in the climate of every region on Earth. More time is needed to determine if a period of increasing warm weather is permanent or temporary.

■ **Experiment**

Now, start experimenting with how the physical characteristics of surface materials affect climate.

Hints

☐ Glass, much like greenhouse gases, allows sunlight to pass through but traps infrared radiation.

☐ Design an experiment to test the effects of surface materials with different physical characteristics, such as colored soils, dry and wet soils, grass, green or dry leaves, or different types of coverings such as plastic or aluminum foil.

☐ Design a way to measure the temperature, such as by putting a thermometer inside a closed glass container. Where is the best place to put the thermometer?

Determine the Effect of Changes in Air Pressure on Wind Velocity

■ What You Need to Know

Force is a push or pull on an object. **Air pressure** is the force exerted on any surface by air molecules. **Air pressure gradient** is the difference in air pressure between two neighboring areas. **Pressure gradient force** is the force that causes wind. **Density** is a measure of mass or the number of particles per unit volume.

■ How Does the Pressure Gradient Force Work?

The pushing force of air is called air pressure. As the air pressure increases, the greater is its pushing force. Air pressure varies from one area to another. Winds begin with differences in air pressures. This difference in the pressure between the two neighboring areas is the air pressure gradient, which causes wind. **Meteorologists** (scientists who study the weather) refer to the force that starts the wind flowing as the pressure gradient force. Wind moves from a high air pressure area toward an area with lower air pressure.

■ What Does This Have to Do with Wind Velocity?

Velocity is more than just how fast an object is moving. It also includes the direction of the object. The velocity of wind is its speed and the direction from which it comes. A 5-mile (8 km) per hour south wind means the wind is coming from the south and blowing toward the north. Meteorologists use compass direction to identify the exact direction of wind. Thus a wind direction of 0° means that the wind is blowing from due north. A wind direction of 90° is blowing from due east. A wind direction of 180° is blowing from due south, and 270° is a wind blowing from due west. The arrow in the figure represents a wind with a 45° direction. This means that the wind is blowing from the northeast.

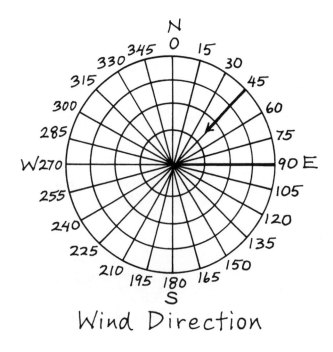

Wind Direction

....

Real-Life Science Challenge

Air masses of different temperatures have different pressures. When such air masses meet, the resulting pressure difference (which causes wind) is highest in the upper atmosphere. Upper atmosphere wind speeds average 35 miles (56 km) per hour in the summer and 75 miles (120km) per hour in the winter, although speeds of over 250 miles (402 km) per hour are known. If the wind speed in the upper atmosphere is higher than 55 miles (88 km) per hour, the wind is called a **jet stream**. Jet streams are usually found somewhere between 6 and 9 miles (10–15 km) above Earth's surface and flow eastward. Since the progress of an airplane is aided by tailwinds and hindered by headwinds, eastbound aircraft try to fly with the jet stream in order to gain speed and save fuel. Westbound aircraft try to avoid the jet stream. The time it takes to fly across the United States from west to east is decreased by about 30 minutes if the aircraft flies with the jet stream or increased by the same amount if it avoids the jet stream.

....

Now, start experimenting with air pressure and velocity.

Hints

□ A glass container such as an aquarium, covered by a lid that has two holes in it, can be used to observe smoke moving in and out of the container due to differences in air pressure.

□ A burning mosquito coil or punt can produce smoke to help you see air movement.

□ Changes in air pressure can be created by changing air density or temperature in a container.

Caution: Have an adult supervise and assist you in heating something to create smoke.

Fun Fact

Air pressure affects the temperature at which water boils. At sea level, the temperature at which water boils is generally 212° F (100° C). But at high elevations, such as in the mountains, where the air pressure is lower, water boils at a lower temperature. This means that at higher elevations food does not heat as quickly, and it takes longer to cook it.

Determine How Earth's Rotation Affects the Spin Direction of Hurricanes

■ **What You Need to Know**

Wind is the horizontal flow of air relative to Earth's surface. The **Coriolis effect** is the apparent deflection of free-moving things due to the rotation of the Earth. To **deflect** means to turn aside from a straight path. A **hurricane** is a tropical cyclone with a constant wind speed of 74 miles (119 km) per hour or more. A **cyclone** is an area of low atmospheric pressure around which spiraling winds blow. The **tropics** is a band about 3,000 miles (4,800 km) wide around the equator.

■ **How Does the Coriolis Effect Work?**

Differences in air pressure between two areas tend to push air in a straight path. But as the air moves from a high-pressure area to a low-pressure area, Earth rotates under it, making the wind appear

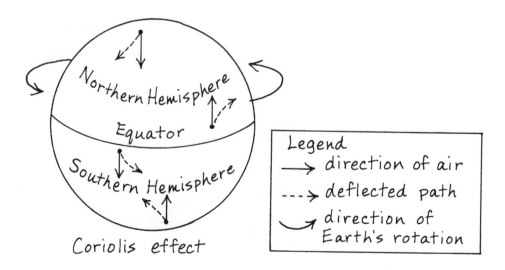

Coriolis effect

to follow a curved path. In the Northern Hemisphere, wind deflects to the right of its direction of motion. In the Southern Hemisphere, wind deflects to the left. These apparent deflections are called the Coriolis effect.

What Does This Have to Do with the Spin Direction of Hurricanes?

The Coriolis effect causes winds to deflect to the right in the Northern Hemisphere, but in hurricanes wind spins counterclockwise around a low-pressure area north of the equator. This happens because while wind is deflected to the right by the Coriolis effect, air-pressure difference is pushing the air toward the center of the area of low pressure. The diagram below shows the counterclockwise movement of air around a low-pressure area in the Northern Hemisphere. The solid arrow represents the force on the air due to pressure differences. The spiraling solid line shows the resulting counterclockwise wind motion.

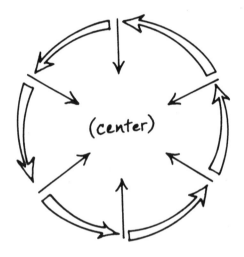

Hurricane winds
in Northern Hemisphere

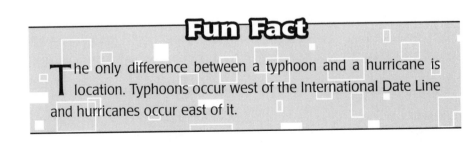

Real-Life Science Challenge

At this time, scientists can track only the direction and wind speed of an existing typhoon or hurricane. This information is broadcast to the public so that people in the storm's potential path can prepare. A storm is put in a category from 1 to 5 depending on its wind speed and the potential damage it may cause when it hits land. These categories are:

Category	Wind Speed (gust in km/h)	Damage Potential
1	Gale (119–153)	Minimal
2	Storm (154–177)	Moderate
3	Hurricane (178–209)	Major
4	Hurricane (210–249)	Devastating
5	Hurricane (>249)	Extreme

■ Experiment

Now, start experimenting with the deflection of a moving object due to rotation. Why do hurricanes spin counterclockwise north of the equator and clockwise south of the equator?

Hints

☐ A revolving surface, such as a lazy Susan, can be used to simulate the Earth's rotation.

☐ Moving a pencil or a pen in a straight line across a paper secured to a revolving surface is one way of recording the path of a moving object due to rotation.

☐ Research other methods of recording the deflected path of a moving object on a rotating surface.

Design a Device That Makes a Vertical Line

What You Need to Know

In relation to Earth, **horizontal** is a direction that is parallel with the horizon, which is a left/right position. **Perpendicular** means at a right angle to a plane or a surface. **Vertical** is a direction that is in an up/down position, which is perpendicular to the horizon.

How Does a Perpendicular Line Work?

A horizontal line goes from left to right (or right to left). A tabletop has a horizontal surface. Vertical describes a line or an object that is perpendicular (at a right angle) to a horizontal surface. For example, boards A and B in the fence diagram are vertical, and boards C and D are horizontal. This means that boards A and B are perpendicular to boards C and D, and vice versa. To indicate that lines are perpendicular to each other, a square can be drawn in the corner where the lines meet. Two of the sixteen right angles formed by the boards are identified. Can you find the others?

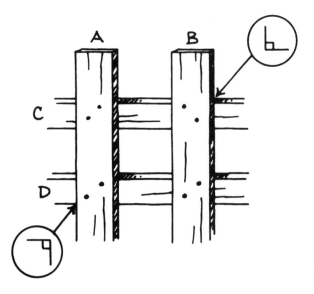

Fun Fact

Gravity pulls everything, including you, toward the center of the Earth. No matter where you stand on Earth, such as at the North Pole or the South Pole, the ground beneath you is down and the sky overhead is up.

■ What Does This Have to Do with Making a Vertical Line?

Gravity pulls everything toward the center of the Earth. A line pointing toward the center of the Earth would be a vertical line. Carpenters can use this fact to determine that a building is perfectly vertical. What is a plumb bob?

....

Real-Life Science Challenge

Carpenters use a device called a **level** to determine how straight a structure is. A level has a tube of liquid with a small bubble in it. When the level is held against the side of a building, the bubble in the level will be in the center of the tube if the wall is vertical. If you turn the level so that it is horizontal, it will tell you if a floor is truly horizontal. The bubble in the level will be in the center of the tube if the floor is horizontal.

....

■ Experiment

Now, start experimenting with a device that makes a vertical line.

Hints

☐ Free-hanging objects hang vertically if wind or another force does not move them.

☐ Weighted objects resist motion.

Find as Many Real-Life Examples of Mechanical Weathering as Possible

■ **What You Need to Know**

Weathering is the process by which rocks are broken into smaller pieces. **Mechanical weathering** is weathering that physically breaks rocks through direct contact with outside forces. **Abrasion** is a type of mechanical weathering that involves the breaking of rocks by a grinding action. **Exfoliation** is weathering that involves the removal of the surface layers of a rock. **Erosion** is a two-step process by which materials are worn away. Step one is weathering, and step two is the removal of the particles.

■ **How Does Mechanical Weathering Work?**

One example of abrasion is when rock surfaces are ground away by sand grains that are carried by wind or water. Unusual rock formations can be created when softer surfaces, such as sandstone, are eroded.

Temperature also causes mechanical weathering. Water that has filled cracks in a rock can break the rock when the water expands as it freezes. Changes in the temperature of the rock itself can also cause it to break apart. During the day, heat from the sun warms rocks, causing them to expand. At night the rocks cool and contract. This repeated expansion and contraction weakens them, and their top layers can crack and peel off in curved sheets parallel to the surface of the rock. This is called exfoliation. Another example of weathering by an expanding surface is the growth of a seed. If a seed falls into a crack in a rock, the expanding seed can force the crack to widen. Eventually, as the plant grows, the rock can break apart.

Sandstone formations

■ **What Does This Have to Do with Finding Examples of Mechanical Weathering?**

By knowing what causes mechanical weathering, you have clues where to look. For example, as the roots of plants grow they can break rocks apart. Look for a tree growing close to a concrete sidewalk or moss growing on a rock and you may find cracks caused by these plants.

Also look for evidence of weathering in places where sand is carried by wind or water and in places where temperatures vary between freezing and warming.

Fun Fact

Weathering produces the particles that soil is made from. It may take 250 to 2,500 years for 1 inch (2.5 cm) of soil to form through weathering.

Real-Life Science Challenge

Mechanical weathering can be used to keep stone buildings clean. Machines that shoot sand at high speed, called sand-blasters, use mechanical weathering to grind the dirt layer off of the stone revealing a nice clean layer underneath.

■ **Experiment**

Now, start finding examples of weathering.

Hints

☐ Observe rocks in areas where a new road is being built.

☐ Observe rocks in sidewalks or rock walls.

☐ Observe rocks at the beach or in streams where water washes over them.

☐ Observe rocks in areas where there is a lot of wind.

101 ■ ■ ■

Find Ways to Keep Leaching from Polluting Water Sources

What You Need to Know

Potable water is water that is safe to drink. The downward flow of water through the spaces that are in soil is called **percolation**. **Runoff** is water that does not get absorbed by the soil; instead, it flows across the ground. **Nitrate** is a type of chemical substance that contains nitrogen, which is necessary for plant growth. **Leaching** is the process by which nutrients in soil are dissolved in water and carried away. **Groundwater** is water that is found below the ground surface.

How Does Leaching Work?

When the spaces between soil particles become filled with water, gravity pulls the water down through the soil. This is called percolation. The water that is not absorbed by the soil runs across its surface, and is called runoff. In both methods of water movement, chemical substances in the soil, such as nitrates, dissolve in the water and are carried away. This movement of water and dissolved materials is called leaching.

Fun Fact

In tropical rain forests, very little nutrients accumulate in the soil. This is because they are quickly absorbed by plants or leached away by rain. Because the soil of tropical rain forests is so nutrient-poor, areas that are cleared for growing **crops** (plants grown for food) are soon not very productive.

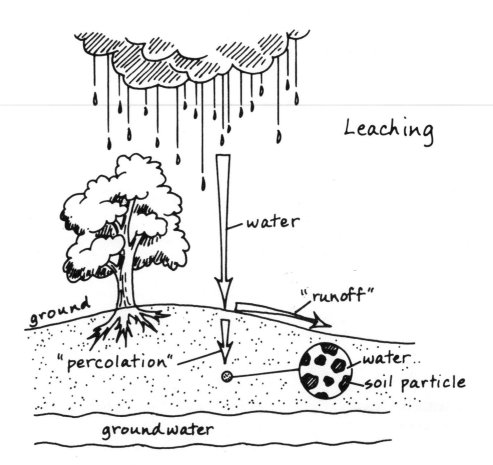

Leaching

water

"runoff"

ground

"percolation"

water
soil particle

groundwater

▪ What Does This Have to Do with Chemicals Polluting Water Sources?

Chemical substances, such as fertilizers and pesticides, leached out of the soil due to percolation can mix with and pollute groundwater. Chemical substances leached out of the soil by runoff can drain into rivers, lakes, or streams and pollute the water.

Real-Life Science Challenge

In areas where nitrates tend to be leached from the soil, other forms of nitrogen fertilizers, such as ammonium, can be used. Unlike nitrate, ammonium tends to attach to the soil particles and resists being leached by moving water.

▪ Experiment

Now, start experimenting with ways to keep leaching from polluting water sources.

Hints

☐ Food coloring can be used to represent chemicals in the soil.

☐ Does the type of soil affect the amount of leaching?

☐ How do different plants affect leaching?

Grow Large Crystals

■ **What You Need
to Know**

A **crystal** is a solid in which the particles are packed in an ordered, repeating pattern. **Precipitate** is the process by which a solid falls out of a solution. **Precipitation** is the solid that precipitates.

■ **How Does a
Crystal Work?**

A crystal is a solid made of repeating units of a substance. These units are in an organized pattern. Because of this organization, crystals of different substances have specific shapes. For example, a crystal of table salt, which is made of units of the chemical sodium chloride, has a cube shape.

■ **What Does This Have
to Do with Growing
Crystals?**

There is an attractive force between the particles in a solid. When solids are dissolved in water, they separate into individual particles. In a solution, these particles are evenly spread throughout the solvent particles. However, occasionally two solute particles are near each other. There will be some attractive force between these solute particles, and they will stick together. Generally, other forces cause them to separate. But if they stay together, they have a greater attractive force than do single particles. As a result a third solute particle sticks to them, then a fourth, and so on, until this cluster of particles, a crystal, can no longer remain dissolved, and it precipitates. If particles of solute continue to stick to the crystal's surface, the crystal grows. Crystal growth is much like stacking equal-size blocks. The shape of the blocks and how they fit together determines the shape of the crystal formed.

Fun Fact

Diamonds are crystals made of carbon atoms. Coal is also a type of crystal made of carbon atoms. The difference between these two crystals is how the carbons stick together.

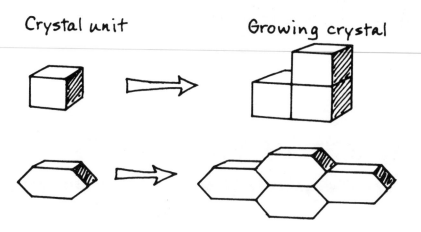

Crystal unit   Growing crystal

Real-Life Science Challenge

Proteins are very important body chemicals necessary for life. Unique chemical structures give each type of protein its own shape and determine its function. Chemical structures that stick out of proteins allow them to interact with other proteins and chemicals in an organism. By studying protein crystals, scientists can better understand the way proteins work. This knowledge could help scientists understand illnesses and develop more effective medicines. However, the structure of many proteins still remains a mystery because scientists are not able to grow these protein crystals large enough to examine.

Experiment

Now, start experimenting with growing crystals.

Caution: Ask for adult supervision if a solution needs to be heated.

Hints

☐ Find information on different types of crystals.

☐ Determine which crystal solutes fall out of a solution more easily.

☐ Try different methods of growing crystals, such as using a surface where crystals may grow.

Determine What Factors Affect the Growth Rate of Crystals

■ **What You Need to Know**

Stalactites are rock structures that hang from the roof of a cave. **Stalagmites** are rock structures that stick up from the floor of a cave and are directly under stalactites. The sheetlike, layered deposits on the walls or floors of caves are called **flowstones**. A **column** is a vertical structure that forms when a stalactite and a stalagmite join together. **Limestone** is a rock made of calcium carbonate. **Calcite** is a type of crystal made of calcium carbonate.

■ **How Do Stalactites and Stalagmites Work?**

A stalactite is a long, icicle-shaped structure that hangs from the roof of a cave. Stalactites form when rainwater containing carbon dioxide from the air combines with limestone. As this liquid mixture percolates through the roof of a cave, some of it falls to the cave floor

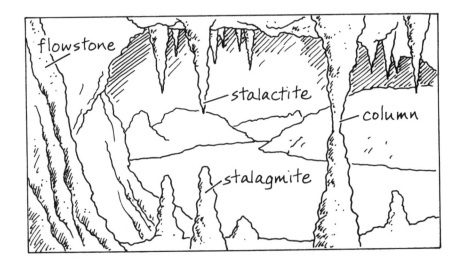

below, some wets the ceiling of the cave, and some dissolves the limestone. When the water evaporates small particles of calcium carbonate, generally in the form of calcite, are left clinging to the ceiling. Over a long period of time, the calcite deposit builds up, eventually forming a stalactite. Drops of mineral-rich liquid that fall from the end of a stalactite produce a mound of calcite projecting up from the cave floor, forming a stalagmite. When the stalactite and the stalagmite touch, a column is formed. The mineral-rich liquid that runs down the walls of the cave produces layer upon layer of calcite that hardens to form flowstone.

What Does This Have to Do with the Growth Rate of Crystals?

Because of the amount of dripping water in a cave, the humidity in the cave is high. Does humidity affect crystal growth? What about temperature? Caves are cool. At a lower temperature, water evaporates slower. Does the evaporation rate affect crystal growth?

Real-Life Science Challenge

Different kinds of crystals are always needed for new technological devices such as computers and cellular phones. Crystal growth is also studied in the medical field. For example, by modeling the crystal formation of kidney stones, scientists can better understand how these crystals **aggregate** (cluster together) and attach to kidney cells. This research not only will provide important information that may prove useful for preventing kidney stone disease but also for other related diseases that are caused by similar crystal formation.

Experiment

Now, start experimenting with factors that affect the growth rate of crystals.

Hints

☐ Solutes that form crystals by water evaporation include table salt found at the grocery store, and Epsom salts and alum found at the pharmacy.

☐ Temperature can be increased using sunlight or decreased by placing experiment materials in a refrigerator.

Make a Model of Earth's Water Cycle

■ **What You Need to Know**

The **water cycle** is the process by which water moves back and forth between Earth and the atmosphere. **Precipitation** is any form of water that falls from the atmosphere and reaches Earth's surface.

■ **How Does Precipitation Work?**

Water from the surface of bodies of water, including oceans, lakes, ponds, and even mud puddles, evaporates, and the gas that is formed mixes with the air in Earth's atmosphere. Evaporation occurs when a liquid gains enough energy for the particles on its surface to break away. Large amounts of water are also added to the atmosphere daily by transpiration. During transpiration, water that is taken in by the roots of plants is lost from the plants' leaves by evaporation. A small amount of the water that is added to the atmosphere is from the exhaled breath of people and animals.

Condensation is the opposite of evaporation. Condensation is the change of a gas to a liquid and occurs when a gas is cooled. In the atmosphere, the water droplets formed from condensation are so small that they float in the air. Millions of these floating water droplets form clouds. The small water droplets that make up clouds form only when water vapor and small dust particles are present around which the droplet can form. Water droplets in clouds form larger drops that fall in the form of rain. Clouds rarely form in the atmosphere above a desert region because there is very little water to evaporate. Coastal regions have many clouds. Depending on the temperature, precipitation may be liquid raindrops or solid snowflakes, sleet, or hail.

Much of the water that falls as precipitation forms runoff that moves across Earth's surface into lakes, streams, and rivers, and some eventually returns to the ocean. The rest of the water moves down through soil and rock. Some of this water remains below ground, and some returns to the surface in springs. Water evaporates from springs, rivers, lakes, and oceans, and the water cycle begins again.

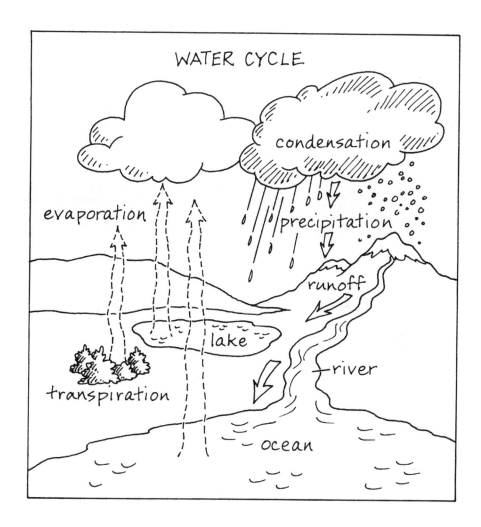

Real-Life Science Challenge

During the continuous movement of water in the water cycle, water can take many pathways. Some water is captured in polar ice for millions of years. Some soaks into the soil and is used by plants or percolates down to groundwater, which in time returns to the surface and evaporates. People can temporarily divert water from the water cycle by pumping it from natural sources and storing it for use. In time, used water is returned to the cycle. Scientists called **hydrologists** study the flow of water in the water cycle, and one of their challenges is to determine ways to improve the quality of used water.

....

■ **Experiment**

Now, start experimenting with ways to model the water cycle.

Hints

☐ Research all of the elements that contribute to the water cycle.

☐ See-through plastic boxes with lids can create a closed system that you can observe.

☐ Ice placed on the outside surface of the closed container can cause condensation of water vapor resulting in precipitation.

Fun Fact

Even though water is constantly changing from one form to another, the total amount of water on Earth remains constant. The water particles that dinosaurs drank still exist today.

Determine the Effect of Wind on Measuring Rainfall

■ **What You Need to Know**

A **gauge** is a scale of measurement. A **rain gauge** is a device used to collect and measure rainfall.

■ **How Does a Rain Gauge Work?**

Rainfall measurement is the depth of accumulated rainfall in a period of time. Because rain generally sinks into the ground, runs off the surface into streams, collects in low areas, or evaporates, the amounts of rainfall cannot be measured with accuracy in natural places. Instead, a rain gauge is used. A rain gauge is usually a cylinder with a scale in inches or millimeters on its side. The diagram below shows two types of rain gauges, one with a funnel-shape top and the other with straight sides.

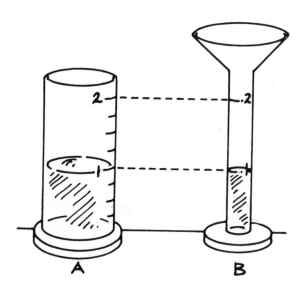

For a gauge like rain gauge A, the actual height of the rain collected in the cylinder is equal to the amount of rainfall. Rain gauge A shows 1 inch (2.5 cm) of water, thus the rainfall measurement is 1 inch (2.5 cm). Rain gauges with funnels, like rain gauge B, are used to collect and measure small amounts of rainfall. In gauges with a funnel top, the height of the water in the cylinder does not equal the amount of rainfall. Instead, the ratio of the diameter of the cylinder to the diameter of the funnel is used to make the measurement. To determine the amount of rainfall per 1 division on the scale of the rain gauge: (1) write down the ratio, (2) express the ratio as a fraction, and (3) divide the denominator of the fraction into the numerator. For example, if the ratio is 1:10, the scale would be determined as follows:

1:10 = 1 inch of rainfall/10 inch height of water in the cylinder
= 0.1 inch of rainfall / 1 inch height of water in the cylinder

Rainfall is usually described as either light, moderate, or heavy. Light rainfall is less than 0.10 inches (0.25 cm) of rain per hour. Moderate rainfall measures 0.10 to 0.30 inches (0.25 to 0.85 cm) of rain per hour, and heavy rainfall is more than 0.30 inches (0.85 cm) of rain per hour.

■ What Does This Have to Do with the Effect of Wind on Measuring Rainfall?

A rain gauge measures the amount of rainfall in a specified period of time. This means the amount of rain that would accumulate on a level surface if none of the rain soaked in, ran off, or evaporated. Catching rain that falls vertically is not a problem. But what about rain that is being blown by the wind and falls at an angle? Does this affect the amount collected?

Fun Fact

One inch (2.5 cm) of rainfall produces 4.7 gallons (17.9 L) of water per square yard or 22,650 gallons (86,070 L) of water per acre.

Real-Life Science Challenge

It's a challenge to measure rainfall at sea where it must be measured on ships. The motion of the ship presents a problem. Special rain gauges have been designed to improve the accuracy of rainfall measurement on moving ships, but better methods are still needed.

■ Experiment

Now, start experimenting with determining the effect of wind on measuring rainfall.

Hints

☐ Design and build a rain gauge.
☐ A spray mister can be used to simulate rainfall.
☐ A fan can be used to simulate wind.

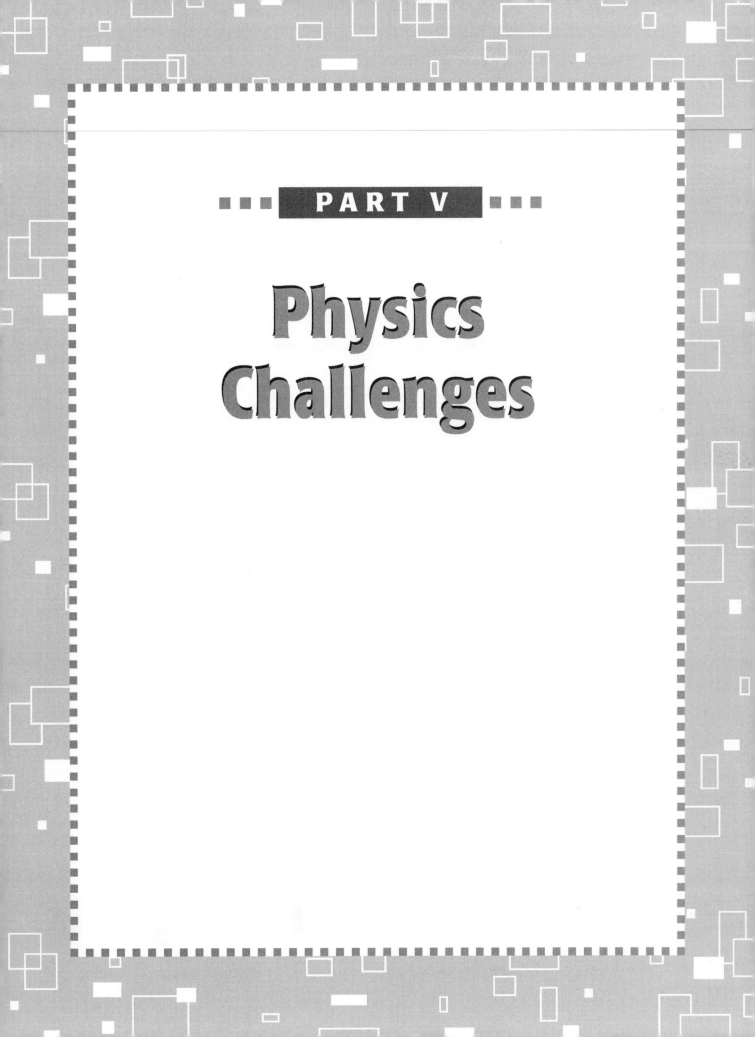

PART V

Physics Challenges

Find Ways to Reduce Friction

What You Need to Know

Force is a push or pull on an object. **Friction** is the force that opposes the motion of objects whose surfaces are in contact with each other. A **ball bearing** is a sphere that not only supports but also rotates in order to reduce friction between moving parts. A **lubricant** is a substance used to reduce the friction between two solid surfaces.

How Does Friction Work?

Friction is a force that resists motion. The amount of friction depends on how an object is moved, such as by sliding it or rolling it. When two things slide, the friction between them is greater than if they roll over each other. For example, it would be much more

difficult to pull a wagon on grass if it had skis instead of wheels. In the figure on page 115, muscle force is used to pull the wagon. At the same time, the force of friction between the skis and the surface they move across, the grass, is trying to make the wagon stop. As the force of friction increases, more force is needed to move the wagon. The amount of friction also depends on how rough or smooth the surfaces of the objects moved are. The wagon with skis would be much easier to pull on snow because the surface of the snow is smooth. When things in contact move, the rougher their surfaces the greater the friction.

What Does This Have to Do with Ways to Reduce Friction?

There are many ways to reduce friction between objects. Lubricants, such as oil, reduce friction by filling in surfaces, making them smoother. Ball bearings rotate to reduce friction between objects by changing sliding friction to rolling friction.

Fun Fact

The osprey is the only hawk that hunts in water. It looks for fish that feed at the surface of the water. When the osprey is airborne, it turns the captured fish headfirst, which reduces air friction as it flies. Its claws also have spiky Velcrolike pads that increase friction and help the bird keep a firm grasp on a slippery wet fish.

Real-Life Science Challenge

Even though friction opposes motion, it also helps objects to start moving. For example, friction between a bicycle tire and a road helps the tire to grip (to hold onto) the road. If the road is covered with ice, there is so little friction between the tire and the ice that the tire slips and spins freely, and the bicycle is not able to move. Engineers are challenged to design tires with many features, including high **static friction** (the bonding of two objects at rest) and low **rolling friction** (the friction between a rolling object and a surface). The tires must also flex to fit road irregularities and yet be rigid enough to minimize heat buildup. These are accomplished by choice of materials, tire design, tread design, inflation pressure, and many other factors.

■ Experiment

Now, start experimenting with friction. How can it be reduced?

Hints

☐ Design a method for measuring friction such as:

- The rate at which objects move.
- The amount of force it takes to move objects using a spring scale or a scale you designed.

☐ Test different methods for reducing friction on a specific object.

Compare the Viscosity of Different Fluids

■ **What You Need to Know**

A **fluid** is a gas or a liquid. The measurement of how easily a fluid flows is called **viscosity**.

■ **How Does Viscosity Work?**

Friction is a force that opposes the motion of objects that are in contact with one another. For a fluid to flow, its particles must move across one another. So viscosity is a measure of the friction among the particles of a fluid.

■ **What Does This Have to Do with Finding the Viscosity of Different Fluids?**

The greater the friction among the particles of a fluid, the greater is the viscosity and the slower is the motion of the fluid. For example, the frictional forces among the particles in honey are much greater than the frictional forces among the particles in water. So the viscosity of honey is greater than the viscosity of water. Thickness is also an indication of viscosity. The more viscous the fluid, the thicker it is. Honey is more viscous and thicker than water. Another observation of high viscosity is how smoothly a liquid pours. When thick honey is poured into a bowl, it pours smoothly, while thinner water, with a much lower viscosity, splashes about.

honey

water

Real-Life Science Challenge

Many fluids get thicker and more viscous when they get colder and thinner and less viscous when they are heated. The viscosity of multiweight motor oil used in cars is specified using two numbers, such as 10W30. The first number, 10, is the viscosity of the oil when it is cold. The letter W stands for winter. The number 30, after the W, indicates the viscosity of the oil when it is at operating temperature. The higher the number, the thinner the oil.

Multiweight motor oil is used in order to protect an engine at start time, when the cold oil needs to be thinner. Because cold oil is normally thicker than hot oil, chemicals are added to make the oil thinner when it is cold, without making the oil too thin when it heats up. This kind of oil has particles connected in chains. When the oil is cold, the chains ball up, reducing the forces between them, so the oil doesn't get too thick. When the oil is hot, the particle chains stretch out and the forces between them increase, preventing the oil from getting too thin at higher temperatures. The multiweight oil 10W30 is thicker when it is cold than is the multiweight oil 5W30.

■ Experiment

Now, start experimenting with the viscosity of different fluids.

Hints

☐ Try comparing different fluids, such as honey, ketchup, and water.

☐ Test the viscosity of the fluids at different temperatures.

Caution: Have an adult supervise you if you are heating fluids.

Fun Fact

The lower the viscosity of *magma* (liquid rock) in an active volcano the higher the possibility it will erupt. This is because it takes less pressure to push the thin magma to the surface than it would take for thick magma. However, if an eruption occurs with high-viscosity magma, it results in a huge explosion. This is because it takes so much force to push the thicker magma out of the volcano.

Create a Balloon Rocket

■ What You Need to Know

A **law** is a scientific statement that is generally accepted as true. **Newton's third law of motion** says that for every action force there is an equal and opposite reaction force.

■ How Does Newton's Third Law of Motion Work?

Sir Isaac Newton (1642–1727) realized that if one object applies a force on another, the second object applies the same amount of force on the first object but in an opposite direction. Since these forces are not opposed, they are said to be unbalanced. Unbalanced forces cause the objects they push against to move in the direction of the force. The diagram on the left shows Newton's third law in action. When the boy hits the golf ball with the golf club, the ball is pushed forward, and the golf club is pushed backward. Two forces, A and B as shown, are needed to make these movements. Notice that the arrows for the forces are equal in size, are in opposite directions, and are on different objects. Force A is from the club hitting the ball, and force B is from the ball hitting the club. You can be sure that two forces are action-reaction pairs of forces if the

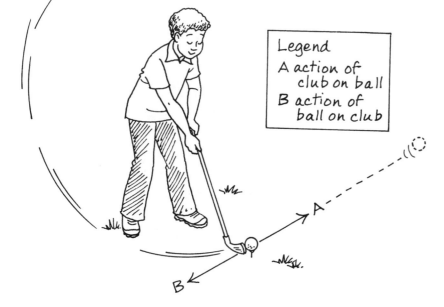

Legend
A action of
   club on ball
B action of
   ball on club

reverse description of one force describes the other. In the figure, the identified action-reaction pair is A/B. The description of force A is "the club pushes against the ball," and the description of force B is "the ball pushes against the club."

■ What Does This Have to Do with Creating a Balloon Rocket?

If an inflated balloon with an open end is released, the balloon will fly through the air due to the unbalanced forces making up action/reaction pairs of forces. In the diagram below, one set of action/reaction forces (A/B) is shown. Force A is on the balloon due to the gas inside the balloon pushing on the wall of the balloon. Force B is on the gas due to the balloon pushing on the gas inside the balloon. Because of these unbalanced forces, the gas is pushed out of the balloon and the balloon is pushed forward.

Legend
↑ A action force
↓ B reaction force
∴ air particles

. . . .

Real-Life Science Challenge

How does a rocket fly through empty space? Like the balloon, real rockets do not move because the exhaust gas pushes against the ground or air surrounding the craft. Instead, a rocket moves because of the unbalanced forces in action/reaction pairs. That's why rockets move in space where there is nothing for the exhaust gas to push against.

. . . .

Now, start experimenting with your balloon rocket. What kind of balloon rocket goes the fastest? What kind goes the farthest? What effect do balloon size and shape have on the rocket's flight?

Hints

☐ Design a way to control the direction of the balloon rocket's flight. For example, you could run a string through a straw, then stretch the string between two objects, such as chairs. Tape the balloon to the straw.

☐ What else can make your balloon go farther, faster, or straighter?

Build a Toy That Will Throw a Ball toward a Target

■ What You Need to Know

Energy is the ability an object has to do work. **Work** is the product of force times the distance. It moves an object in the direction of that force. **Mechanical energy** is the total kinetic and potential energy of an object. **Kinetic energy** is the energy an object has because of its motion. **Potential energy** is the energy an object has because of its position, also called stored energy. **Energy transfer** is the change of one form of energy to another.

■ How Does Energy Do Work?

An object with mechanical energy is able to do work. An object's mechanical energy enables it to apply a force to another object causing it to move. The amount of force applied times the distance the object moves equals the amount of work done on the object. In the process of doing work, the object doing the work transfers mechanical energy to the object upon which work is done.

The toy in the diagram on page 124 is an example of how mechanical energy of an object can do work. When the spring is compressed, it possesses mechanical energy in the form of potential energy. When the compressed spring separates, the potential energy in the spring is changed to kinetic energy, and the toy moves as in figure B.

■ What Does This Have to Do with Building a Toy That Will Throw a Ball toward a Target?

Your toy must be able to store and transfer energy in some way so that it can throw a ball in a certain direction. You can start the toy by squeezing a spring together or stretching a rubber band, for example, but it must be the toy that throws the ball. It cannot be your energy that directly moves the ball.

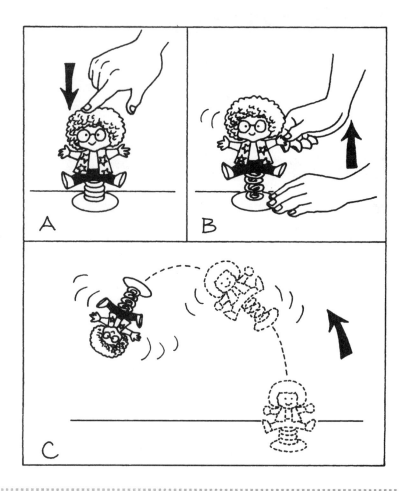

Real-Life Challenge

Oil is used to produce fuels, which are forms of potential energy. Fuel in a car is burned, changing it into different forms of energy that make the car move. When gasoline is burned, it produces gases that pollute the air. Scientists are exploring alternative energy sources. Hybrid cars are examples of machines that use alternative energy sources. The energy sources for these cars are gasoline and electricity. The electricity is stored in a rechargeable battery, which recharges as the car is driven.

Experiment

Now, start experimenting with toys that store and transfer energy.

Hints

- Research the motion of different kinds of simple machines, such as wheels and gears.
- Study the motion of toys. Determine the type of simple machines involved.

Determine the Effect of Temperature on How High a Rubber Ball Bounces

What You Need to Know

Elasticity is the ability of a material to return to its original length, shape, or size immediately after a deforming force has been removed. A **bond** is an attractive force between atoms.

How Does Elasticity Work?

Elastic materials are things that can be bent, stretched, or squeezed and then return to their original size or shape. For example, when you stretch a rubber band, it returns to its original shape when you release it. How elastic a material is depends on how much the atoms can be separated without breaking the bonds between them.

What Does This Have to Do with How Temperature Affects a Ball's Bounce?

When a ball is dropped, gravity pulls it toward the ground. As the ball falls, its potential energy changes to kinetic energy (energy of motion). When the ball hits the ground, it stops, and its kinetic energy goes into deforming the ball. Some of the ball's molecules are stretched apart and some are squeezed together. This changes the ball's original round shape to a squashed shape.

Fun Fact

Rubber balls have been found that date as early as 1600 B.C. These balls were made from natural rubber mixed with different plant juices, including the sap from morning glories. Like today's modern rubber, these mixtures produce a bouncy substance, but it is not as temperature resistant.

The squashed ball has potential energy because the elastic material the ball is made of makes it regain its round shape. This is due to the energy transfer from potential energy to kinetic energy. Thus, a shape change from flat to round pushes the ball back up.

Real-Life Science Challenge

Natural rubber is plant sap, particularly from the tree *Hevea brasiliensis*. Natural rubber becomes soft and sticky when hot, and hard and brittle when cold, so it isn't very good for making things. Between 1830 and 1839, the American inventor Charles Goodyear (1800–1860) solved this problem. After many unsuccessful attempts at making rubber that was useful at a wide range of temperatures, he accidentally dropped a mixture of rubber and sulfur on a hot stove. Instead of melting, the mixture charred. He called this process **vulcanization**. Today synthetic rubber, called neoprene, is used to make tires, wet suits, seals and gaskets, hoses, and many other products.

■ **Experiment**

Now, start experimenting by comparing the bounce of rubber balls that are at different temperatures.

Hints

☐ Balls that do not have to be inflated are best. This eliminates the variable of inflation.
☐ Balls can be cooled in a refrigerator or heated in sunlight. (*Caution:* Do not heat balls by any other method.)
☐ Work out a way to measure the height of the ball's bounce.

Determine if a Swing Will Move Faster with a Lighter Person on It

What You Need to Know

A **pendulum** is a weight hung so that it swings about a fixed point. The hanging weight of a pendulum is called the **bob**. **Frequency** is the number of swings that a pendulum makes per second. Potential energy is the energy a stationary (nonmoving) object has because of its position or condition. Kinetic energy is the energy an object has because it is moving.

How Does a Pendulum Work?

A simple pendulum is made of a weight at the end of a material, such as a string, a rope, or a rod. When a pendulum hangs vertically, it is said to be at its resting point. In the diagram on the left, the bob (the metal washer) is pulled to side A. When the bob is released, gravity causes the pendulum to swing back and forth between positions A and C. The transfer between potential and kinetic energy keeps the pendulum swinging, and the friction between the pendulum and the air causes it to slow and finally stop. One back-and-forth movement from A to C is equal to one swing. Frequency is measured in swings per time. The formula to use to calculate frequency is F = swings/time. For example, if the pendulum makes 10 swings in 5 seconds, its frequency is:

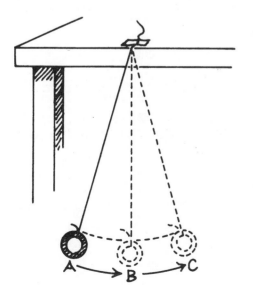

F = 10 swings/5 seconds

= 2 swings/second

This is read as 2 swings per second.

What Does This Have to Do with How Fast a Swing Moves?

A swing is an example of a pendulum. The bob for this pendulum is the seat and the person on it. So the weight of the bob changes with the weight of the person sitting on the seat. When the swing is pulled to one side and then released, gravity pulls it down and it continues to move back and forth for a while. The swing is falling because of the pull of gravity, and the ropes attached to it cause it to move in a curved path. If the size of the bob doesn't change, and it is pulled to the side the same distance each time, will changing its weight affect its frequency?

Fun Fact

One of the largest pendulum clocks in the world is 97 feet (29 m) tall, which is about as high as a 5- or 6-story building. While this pendulum clock is very large, it looks small compared to the building to which it is attached, the 810-foot (243 m) twin tower railroad station in Tokyo, Japan.

Real-Life Science Challenge

Two things needed to make a clock include a way to mark off equal amounts of time and a way of keeping track of and displaying the amount of time. Around 1582, Galileo Galilei (1564–1642) observed that, as it moves, a pendulum marks off equal amounts of time. But it was the Dutch scientist Christiaan Huygens (1629–1695) who, in 1656, built the first pendulum clock. His first clock, with an error of less than 1 minute per day, was the first clock to keep such accurate time. A pendulum clock works because the swinging pendulum moves gears inside the clock that move the hands of the clock.

■ Experiment

Now, start experimenting with pendulums and weight. Start with a small pendulum and then compare your results with real-life kids on swings.

Hints

- ☐ Pieces of string with different numbers of washers attached to them can be used as small pendulums.
- ☐ Be sure to vary only the weight. Keep the string length and how far you displace the pendulum the same for each experiment.

Design a Musical Instrument That Can Play Different Pitches

▢ What You Need to Know

Sound is a type of energy that moves through material and causes it to vibrate. **Vibrate** means that a material moves back and forth. A **sound wave** is the pattern in which sound energy travels. **Frequency** is the number of sound waves in a given time. How high or low a sound seems to be is called **pitch**. **Note** refers to a specific pitch.

▢ How Does Sound Work?

Sound is a form of energy, just like electricity and light. Sound energy is produced when molecules vibrate and move in a pattern called sound waves. When sound waves travel through the air to your ears, the waves cause your eardrums to vibrate. The number of sound waves that reach your ears in a given time indicates the frequency. Your brain interprets the frequency of the vibration of your eardrums as a specific sound called pitch. Sounds with a high frequency have a high pitch. In the figure below, the flute produces the sound with the higher pitch.

A   B

What Does This Have to Do with Making a Musical Instrument That Can Play Different Pitches?

Musical instruments are designed to produce different pitches. For example, a guitar has different sizes of strings, and the length of each string can be changed to achieve a certain pitch. The high-pitch strings on a guitar are thinner than the low-pitch strings. Because a high-pitch sound is made by fast vibrations, the thinner the string the faster it vibrates, and the higher the pitch of the sound it produces. The length of the strings also affects their sound. The shorter the strings, the faster they vibrate, producing a higher pitch.

With a wind instrument, such as a flute, covering the openings changes the pitch. This changes the length of the vibrating column of air inside the instrument. Percussion instruments, such as drums, produce sound when they are hit. The pitch varies depending on the space inside the instrument.

Fun Fact

When you hold a large seashell next to your ear, you hear ocean sounds. This is because when sounds outside of the shell enter it, the vibrating air causes the air inside the shell to vibrate. The shape of the inside of the shell affects how the air vibrates, which changes the sound. You do not have to have a seashell to hear ocean sounds; a paper cup will also work. But because the cup has a different shape, the sound will be different.

Real-Life Science Challenge

Exposure to loud sounds for a period of time can cause permanent hearing loss. Tinnitus, which is a persistent ringing in the ears, can be caused by loud sounds. Hearing loss among teens and young adults is on the rise due to their exposure to loud music. More research is needed to determine the negative effects of using technology that produces sound through ear buds or headphones, but it is known that using these devices at high volume puts you at risk for hearing loss.

Experiment

Now, start experimenting with making a musical instrument that can play different pitches.

Hints

☐ Many household items can be turned into musical instruments, such as rubber bands for guitar strings and boxes for drums.

☐ Select one type of instrument and design the instrument so that it produces different pitches.

☐ Identify the musical notes for each pitch.

Use Colored Filters to Send Secret Messages

What You Need to Know

Visible light is light that the human eye can see. The **visible spectrum** includes a list of seven light colors called **hues**. **White light** is light made of all the colors in the visible spectrum. A **filter** is a transparent material that allows only certain hues of light to pass through it.

How Does a Filter Work?

The seven hues of the visible spectrum in order from the least to most energy are: red, orange, yellow, green, blue, indigo, and violet. When combined, the seven hues of light produce white light. The color of an object depends on how the chemicals making up the object's surface absorb or reflect different hues. A filter used to separate light absorbs some hues and allows others to pass through or be reflected. For example, in the diagram on the left, when white light hits the red filter, red, orange, and yellow light pass through it. The filter absorbs the other colors in the white light. The combination of the red, orange, and yellow light is perceived by your eyes as a shade of red.

Sun

red
orange
yellow
green
blue
indigo
violet

white light

red filter

red
orange
yellow

What Does This Have to Do with Using Colored Filters to Send Secret Messages?

A red filter that allows red, orange, and yellow light to pass through it could be used to make words or images appear or disappear. For example, words written in yellow ink on white paper would disappear if a red filter is placed over the writing. The yellow light from the ink blends in with other yellow light passing through the filter. What you see when you look through the filter is a red sheet of paper. The yellow ink seems to have disappeared. Remove the filter and the yellow words appear again. Would the filter cause any shade of red, yellow, or orange ink to disappear?

Fun Fact

The order of the hues in the visible spectrum is the order of the colors in a rainbow. To remember this order, memorize the name ROY G BIV, which is spelled using the first letter of each light color.

Real-Life Science Challenge

Colorblindness is the inability to see some or all colors. While there is no cure for colorblindness, scientists have discovered that colored filters can help with the problem. A red-tinted contact lens can help some colorblind people see certain colors. Recently, tinted prescription eyeglasses that are coated with a colored filter, usually magenta or orange, have become available to people who have trouble distinguishing shades of red and green from other colors. When wearing these glasses, a colorblind person who usually sees a muddy-brown leaf will see a green leaf.

Experiment

Now, start experimenting with filters to send secret messages. Remember that a secret message should be visible under special conditions. The message could be in plain view but camouflaged by its surroundings.

Hints

☐ Transparent, plastic, colored report folders make good filters.

☐ Light-colored felt-tip pens work better for writing secret messages.

Demonstrate the Scattering of Light

■ **What You Need to Know**

Scattering is the deflection or the spreading out of light as it passes through material.

■ **How Does Scattering Work?**

Scattering is different from refraction. Refracted light is deflected in only one direction. Scattering means the light is deflected in all directions. Scattering happens when light energy is absorbed by a particle or a molecule and causes the electrons to be more energized. When the electrons release this extra energy it is in the form of light energy. The released light energy is scattered. Selective scattering occurs when certain particles are more effective at scattering a particular wavelength of light. If particles are small, short-wavelength light is scattered more than long-wavelength light.

■ **What Does This Have to Do with Demonstrating the Scattering of Light?**

Some particles and molecules found in the atmosphere have the ability to scatter sunlight. Air molecules, like oxygen and nitrogen, for example, are small in size and thus more effective at scattering shorter wavelengths of light than are large molecules. The shortest wavelengths of visible light are the colors blue and violet. The scattering of sunlight by air molecules is responsible for producing blue skies. The diagram on page 135 shows the scattering of blue light in all directions by oxygen molecules.

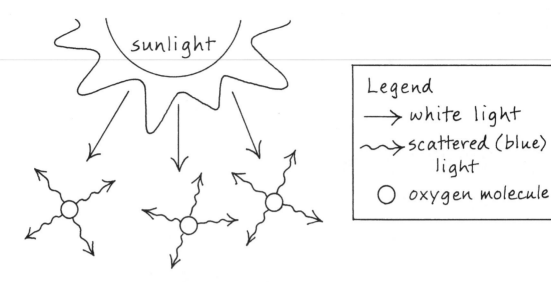

Legend
→ white light
⟿ scattered (blue) light
○ oxygen molecule

Real-Life Science Challenge

Light passing from space through Earth's atmosphere is scattered. Because this light is scattered, it is difficult for scientists using telescopes on Earth to see objects in space. The primary reason for placing the Hubble space telescope in orbit around Earth was to eliminate this undesirable effect of Earth's atmosphere.

■ Experiment

Now, start experimenting with light scattering.

Hints

- ☐ A penlight or other light with a narrow light beam works best as a light source.
- ☐ Investigate Raleigh Scattering experiments, then design a liquid solution to simulate particles in air. Try using small drops of milk or dishwashing soap in water.
- ☐ Design a way to create a screen to observe the color of light that is not scattered but passes through the solution.

Fun Fact

Over the ocean, the scattering of light by salt particles suspended in the air causes brilliant red sunsets. The color is most intense when the sun is closest to the ocean surface because the light passes through more air, and more of the shorter wavelengths are scattered. Red has the longest wavelength so it is not scattered, and more of the red light reaches your eye.

Design a Solar Cooker

What You Need to Know

Solar energy is radiation from the Sun. **Passive solar heating** is a method of heating with solar energy that does not require mechanical power to circulate heat. A **solar cooker** is a device that uses solar energy to cook food.

How Does Passive Solar Heating Work?

Passive solar heating is any method of using energy from sunlight as long as other energy sources, such as electricity, are not used. For example, dark-colored objects absorb more of the sunlight that falls on them than do light-colored objects. Some of the light energy is changed into heat energy, which is also called infrared radiation. Because a black object absorbs more sunlight, it will release more heat than a white object will. Smooth, hard, light-colored objects will reflect more sunlight than rough, soft, dark-colored objects. Passive solar heating can also be achieved by directing the sunlight to a specific place. Light reflects off the surface of shiny objects. Mirrors can be used to focus reflected sunlight, meaning that the mirror directs the sunlight to a specific place.

What Does This Have to Do with a Solar Cooker?

A simple example of solar cooking is making sun tea in a glass jar. The jar is filled with water, and a tea bag is added. Closing the jar helps to keep the heat in, as well as dirt and bugs out of, the jar. Some of the sunlight passing through the glass changes into infrared radiation which warms the water and thus cooks the tea.

Real-Life Science Challenge

Solar energy doesn't cause air pollution, and there is no end to its supply. Compared to fossil fuels, sunlight is a diluted source of energy. This means that it is spread out over a large area. Sunlight is also only available at certain times, and there is less of it on cloudy days and at different times of the year. But ways of collecting and transforming sunlight into other energy forms, including solar cells that change sunlight into electricity, are constantly being improved.

■ **Experiment**

Now, start experimenting with solar cooking.

Hints

☐ Aluminum foil is very reflective and can be shaped to focus light.

☐ Some foods, such as chocolate and marshmallows, can be cooked at low temperatures.

Caution: Do not try to cook raw meat in your solar cooker.

Glossary

abrasion	In reference to **weathering**, it is the breaking of rocks by a grinding action.
absorb	To soak up.
actual size	The true measurement of an object.
adhesion	A bonding force between unlike particles.
adventitious root	A root that grows from somewhere other than the primary root.
aggregate	To cluster together.
air	A mixture of gases in Earth's **atmosphere**.
air pressure	The **force** exerted on any surface by air molecules; usually expressed as the weight of a column of air per unit surface area.
air pressure gradient	The difference in **air pressure** between two neighboring areas.
allelochemical	A special chemical released by some plants to prevent other plants from growing too close to them.
altitude	The height, measured in degrees, of a point in the sky above the horizon.
ambidextrous	The ability to use either hand with equal ease.
aperture	The opening through which light enters an **optical instrument**.
apparent brightness	How bright a **celestial body** appears to be as observed from Earth.
apparent magnitude	The measure of a celestial body's **apparent brightness**.
apparent size	How large an object appears to be from a specific distance.
aqueous solution	A **solution** in which the **solvent** is water.
astrologer	Someone who predicts the future using the position of the Sun, the Earth, the **zodiac constellations**, and other **celestial bodies**.
astrology	The notion that the positions and motions of the stars and planets determine people's personalities and futures.

astronomical unit (AU)	A unit for measuring distance; 1 AU is the average distance from Earth to the Sun, which is about 93 million miles (149 million km).
astronomy	The scientific study of **celestial bodies**.
atmosphere	The layer of air surrounding Earth.
auxin	A chemical in plants that affects plant growth.
averted vision	The method of observing an object by looking off to the side so that light enters the eye and falls on the **rods**.
axis	An imaginary line through the center of an object or the north-to-south line through the center of a celestial sphere from pole to pole about which the body rotates.
ball bearing	A sphere that not only supports but also rotates in order to reduce **friction** between moving parts.
baseline	The distance between the two observing points when measuring the parallax shift of an object.
black water	Toilet water; **sewage**.
blue moon	The second **full moon** that occurs during one month.
bob	The hanging weight of a **pendulum**.
bond	An attractive **force** between atoms.
bract	A special petallike leaf.
calcite	A type of **crystal** made of calcium carbonate.
capillary action	The movement of a liquid, such as water, through very small spaces due to **adhesion** and **cohesion**.
casein	A **polymer** that comes from milk.
celestial body	A natural object in the sky, including the **Sun**, **planets**, moons, and **stars**.
cellulose	The tough material in plant stems.
chemical reaction	The change in the arrangement of particles in one or more substances resulting in the formation of one or more new substances.
chlorophyll	A green **pigment** found in plants.
chromatography	A procedure for separating the parts of a **solution** by the use of an **absorbing** material.
climate	The average weather in a region over a long period of time.
cloning	The process of making an identical copy of an **organism**.
cohesion	A **bonding force** between like particles.
colorblindness	The inability to see some or all of the colors.
column	A **vertical** structure that forms when a **stalactite** and a **stalagmite** join together.
complete flower	A flower that has **sepals**, **petals**, **stamens**, and **pistils**.
composite flower	A flower made of many separate flowers.
concentration	The amount of **solute** dissolved in a **solvent**.
conclusion	A summary of the results of an **experiment** and how they relate to the hypothesis or how it solves the challenge problem.

condensation	The change of a gas to a liquid; the opposite of **evaporation**.
cones	Cells on the back of your eyes used for high-level light that specialize in color perception.
constellation	A group of **stars** that appear to form a pattern in the sky.
contract	To get smaller.
control	An experiment that is used as a standard with which to compare your results.
controlled variable	A **variable** other than an **independent** or **dependent variable** that is not allowed to change.
convex lens	A **lens** that has an outward curved surface and is thicker in the center than at the edge.
Coriolis effect	The apparent deflection of free-moving things due to the rotation of the Earth.
corrosion	In reference to metals, it is the slow eating away of a metal due to a **chemical reaction**.
crops	Plants grown for food.
crystal	A solid in which all the particles it is composed of are packed together in an ordered, repeating pattern.
crystallize	The process by which particles bond together, forming a solid.
cyclone	An area of low atmospheric pressure around which spiraling winds blow.
dark-adapted	In reference to eyes, it is when the pupil is **dilated**, allowing more light to enter.
data	Collected and recorded information.
deflect	To turn aside from a straight path.
dehydration	The excessive loss of water from a substance.
density	A measure of mass or the number of particles per unit volume.
dependent variable	A **variable** you are observing for changes.
diffusion	The movement of particles from one place to another.
dilate	To get larger.
disk flower	A type of flower structure in the **head** of a **composite flower**.
dissolve	In reference to a **solution**, it is the process of the **solute** breaking apart and thoroughly mixing with the **solvent**.
DNA	The material inside the nucleus of every cell that contains the blueprint for all the characteristics of an **organism**.
dominant	In reference to body parts, it is the body part used most.
dormant	Unproductive; inactive.
double convex lens	A **convex lens** with two outward curved surfaces.
double lens	A **lens** that has two curved sides.
ecliptic	The apparent path of the Sun across the sky.
elasticity	The ability of a material to return to its original length, shape, or size immediately after a deforming **force** has been removed.
electron	A negative particle that travels around the nucleus of an atom.

embryo	In reference to seeds, it is the undeveloped plant inside the seed that is in its earliest stages of development.
energy	(1) The ability to cause something to move or change. (2) The ability an object has to do work.
energy transfer	The change of one form of energy to another.
erosion	The two-step process by which land is worn away. Step one is weathering, and step two is the removal of the particle.
escape velocity	The **velocity** an object needs to escape the pull of **gravity** in order to be launched into space.
evaporation	The change of the molecules on the surface of a liquid to a gas.
exfoliation	**Weathering** involving the removal of surface layers of rock.
experiment	The process of testing a **hypothesis**, answering a scientific question, or demonstrating a scientific purpose.
fiber	A hairlike strand of material that is much longer than it is wide.
fiber cells	Plant cells made mostly of **cellulose** and **lignin**.
filter	(1) A **porous** material used to separate parts of a **mixture**. (2) A **transparent** material that allows only certain types of light to pass through it.
filtrate	The liquid that passes through a **filter**.
filtration	A physical process of separating a solid and a liquid by using a **filter**.
flowstone	Sheetlike layered rock deposit on the walls or floors of a cave.
fluid	A gas or a liquid.
focal length	The distance from a **lens** to its **focal point**.
focal point	The point where light rays passing through a **lens** come together.
force	A push or pull on an object.
forensic science	The use of science to investigate physical evidence used in a court of law.
frequency	(1) In reference to a **pendulum**, it is the number of swings that a pendulum makes per second. (2) In reference to **sound**, it is the number of **sound waves** in a given time.
friction	The **force** that opposes the motion of objects whose surfaces are in contact with each other.
full moon	The **moon phase** when the side of the Moon facing the Earth is fully lit.
galvanize	To coat iron with zinc to make it rust-resistant.
gauge	A scale of measurement.
geotropism	The response of plants to **gravity**; also called **gravitropism**.
germination	The process by which seeds begin to grow.
germination inhibitor	A chemical that prevents the **germination** of seeds.
germination starting time	(GST) As defined in this book, it is the time it takes from planting a seed to the first signs of growth.

global warming	A permanent warming change in Earth's climate.
gravity	(1) The force of attraction between all objects in the universe. (2) The **force** that pulls things toward the center of the Earth.
gray water	Waste water from indoors or used household water.
greenhouse effect	The heating that occurs when gases in the **atmosphere** allow sunlight to pass through but trap **infrared radiation** leaving Earth's surface.
groundwater	Water that is found below the ground surface.
hard water	Water that contains high levels of minerals, mostly calcium and magnesium; water that is hard to make suds in.
head	The group of flowers making up a **composite flower**.
homogeneous mixture	A mixture that is the same throughout.
horizon	The line where the sky seems to meet Earth.
horizontal	Parallel with the horizon; a left/right position.
horoscope	A prediction or advice for the future of a person based on the position of planets and signs at a specific time.
Hubble space telescope	A telescope in **orbit** around the Earth.
hues	The seven colors of the **visible spectrum**: red, orange, yellow, green, blue, indigo, and violet.
humidity	The measure of the amount of moisture in the **air**.
hurricane	A tropical **cyclone** with constant wind speed of 74 miles (118 km) per hour or more.
hydrologists	Scientists who study the flow of water in the **water cycle**.
hypothesis	An idea about the solution to a **problem**, based on knowledge and research.
incomplete flower	A flower that lacks **sepals**, **petals**, **stamens**, or **pistils**.
independent variable	A **variable** you change.
inertia	The property of all objects that resists a change in motion or direction.
infrared radiation	Waves of energy that produce heat when absorbed or the heat energy from the Sun that you can't see.
inhibitor	In reference to plants, a chemical that blocks growth.
insoluble	The property of a material that makes it not capable of being mixed with a liquid to form a **solution**.
jet stream	**Wind** speeds higher than 55 miles (88 km) per hour, found 6 to 9 miles (10–15 km) above the Earth, that flow eastward.
kinetic energy	The energy an object has because it is moving.
law	A scientific statement that is generally accepted as true.
leaching	The process by which nutrients in soil are **dissolved** in water and carried away.
lens	A **transparent** object that has either two curved surfaces or one flat surface and one curved surface.
level	A tool used by carpenters to determine how straight a structure is.

light-adapted	In reference to eyes, it is when the pupil is **contracted** to restrict excess light from entering the eye.
light amplification	The process by which objects viewed through an **optical instrument** appear brighter than when viewed with the unaided eye.
light-gathering power	The amount of light an **optical instrument** can collect.
light-year	A unit for measuring distance; 1 light-year is the distance that light will travel in 1 year, which is about 63,000 **AU**.
limestone	A rock made of the chemical substance calcium carbonate.
lubricant	A substance used to reduce **friction** between two solid surfaces.
luminosity	The measure of how much light-energy an object gives off.
luminous	To give off light.
lunar month	The time between two successive and similar **moon phases**; about 29½ days.
magnifying power	The number of times a **lens** can make the size of an image greater than the size of the object being viewed.
mammal	Any of a class of animals with backbones and that nurse their young.
mechanical energy	The total kinetic and potential energy of an object; the ability to do work.
mechanical weathering	**Weathering** that physically breaks rocks through direct contact with outside **forces**.
median	The middle number in a set of numbers.
membrane	A thin, bendable sheet of material.
meteorologist	A scientist who studies the weather.
microorganism	An **organism** that can only be seen with a microscope.
mixture	A combination of two or more substances that can be separated by physical means.
model	A physical representation of something.
moon phase	One of the repeating shapes of the sunlit surface of the Moon as seen from the Earth.
negative geotropism	Plant growth in the opposite direction of the force of gravity.
new moon	The **moon phase** when the side of the Moon facing Earth is not lit.
Newton's third law of motion	A **law** that says that for every action there is an equal and opposite reaction.
night vision	The ability to see in the dark.
nitrate	A type of chemical substance that contains nitrogen.
nonpotable	Not fit for drinking.
note	(1) A musical note is a specific **sound pitch**. (2) A certain scent.
optical illusion	Something that appears different than it really is.
optical instrument	A device, such as a telescope, designed to aid human vision.
orbit	To move in a curved path around another object; the curved path of one object around another.

organism	A living thing.
osmosis	The movement of water through a **membrane** from an area of low **concentration** of **solute** to an area of high concentration of solute.
paper	A thin sheet made from **pulp**.
parallax shift	The apparent change in position of an object when viewed from two different points.
parallel	Lines running side-by-side at an equal distance apart.
passive solar heating	A method of heating with **solar energy** that does not require mechanical power to circulate heat.
path of totality	The region from which a **total solar eclipse** is visible.
pendulum	A weight hung so that it swings about a fixed point.
percolation	The downward flow of water through the spaces in soil.
permeability	The ability of a material to allow a substance to pass through it without affecting the material.
perpendicular	At a right angle to a plane or a surface.
petal	A flower's leaflike structure, often brightly colored, that surrounds and protects the **pistil** and the **stamen**.
pigment	A substance that gives animals and plants color.
pistil	The female part of the flower involved in reproduction.
pitch	How high or low a **sound** seems to be.
planet	A celestial body that **orbits** a sun and shines by reflecting the sun's light.
plant fiber	Natural **fiber** from dead plant cells that are long, narrow, and **tapered**.
Polaris	The North Star.
pollutant	Any unwanted substance.
polymer	A long molecule made up of repeating units linked together by chemical **bonds**.
polyvinyl acetate	A **thermoplastic** polymer.
porous	Having many small holes.
positive geotropism	Plant growth in the direction of the force of gravity.
potable	Drinkable. Water that is safe to drink.
potential energy	The energy a stationary object has because of its position or condition.
precipitate	The process by which a solid falls out of a solution.
precipitation	(1) A solid that falls out of a solution. (2) Any form of water that falls from the **atmosphere** and reaches the Earth's surface.
pressure gradient force	The **force** that causes wind.
principal axis	The line passing through the center of any **lens**.
problem	A scientific question to be solved or a scientific purpose to be demonstrated.
product	The new substance produced in a **chemical reaction**.
propagate	To produce new **organisms**.

pseudoscience	A set of beliefs pretending to be scientific but not based on scientific principles.
pulp	A mixture of water and separated **plant fibers**.
radiation	(1) A type of energy that travels in the form of waves and does not need physical substances to travel. (2) A method by which radiant energy travels.
rain gauge	A device used to collect and measure rainfall.
rate of diffusion	The time it takes for particles to separate and spread evenly in a specific substance.
rate of geotropism	The time it takes for a plant to respond to **gravity**.
rate of osmosis	A measure of the amount of water that moves through a **membrane** in a certain amount of time.
ray flower	A type of flower structure in the **head** of a **composite flower** that often looks like **petals**.
reactant	A starting substance that changes during a **chemical reaction**.
recycle	To process a material so that it can be used again.
refract	To bend or change direction.
research	The process of collecting data about a topic being studied.
residue	The solid material that collects on a **filter**.
reverse osmosis	The opposite of **osmosis**; the movement of water through a **membrane** from an area of high **solute concentration** to an area of low solute concentration.
rods	Cells in the eyes used to detect things that you see in your peripheral vision, especially under low light levels.
rolling friction	Friction between a rolling object and a surface.
rotation	The spinning of an object about its **axis**.
runner	A stem that grows across the surface of the ground.
runoff	Water that does not get **absorbed** by the soil; instead, it flows across the ground.
rust	The **product** of **rusting**; a reddish powder containing iron oxide.
rusticle	A huge, rust-colored, icicle-like mass of rust.
rusting	The common name for the **corrosion** of iron in the presence of water and oxygen.
sap	A watery **solution** with dissolved nutrients that moves through plants.
saturated solution	A **solution** in which no more **solute** can **dissolve**.
scale model	A model made using a ratio between the measurements of the model and the measurements of the object that the model represents.
scanning probe microscope (SPM)	A type of computerized microscope that allows scientists to study atoms on the surface of materials.
scattering	The deflection or the spreading out of light as it passes through material.
science	A system of knowledge about the nature of things in the universe.
science challenge	A science problem that can be solved through investigation.
science fair	An organized contest in which science projects are compared and judged based on predetermined criteria.

scientific method	The process of identifying a problem, thinking through its possible solutions, and testing each possibility for the best solution.
seed coat	The outer covering of a seed.
sepal	A flower's leaflike structure, usually green, that surrounds and protects the flower before it opens.
sewage	Toilet water.
short day plant	A type of plant that requires short periods of daylight and long periods of night in order to flower.
sign	A division of the **zodiac**.
single lens	A **lens** that has one curved side.
slip	A piece of a plant, such as a stem or a leaf, which is capable of growing into a new plant.
soft water	Water that contains little or no calcium and/or magnesium; water that is easy to make suds in.
solar cooker	A device that uses **solar energy** to cook food.
solar energy	Radiation from the Sun.
solar system	A group of **celestial bodies** that **orbit** a **star** called a **sun**.
soluble	Capable of being dissolved.
solute	The dissolved part of a **solution**.
solution	A liquid containing dissolved substances; a combination of a **solute** and a **solvent**.
solvent	The liquid part of a **solution**.
sound	Energy that moves through material, causing it to **vibrate**; vibrations that cause the sense of hearing.
sound wave	The pattern in which **sound** energy travels.
stalactite	A rock structure that hangs from the roof of a cave.
stalagmite	A rock structure that sticks up from the floor of a cave and is directly under a **stalactite**.
stamen	The male part of the flower involved in reproduction.
star	A **celestial body** made of hot gases that gives off energy, including light and heat.
static friction	The bonding of two surfaces when at rest; stationary friction.
stimulus (plural stimuli)	Something that an **organism** responds to.
stoma (plural stomata)	Tiny hole in the surface of a leaf where gases enter and leave a plant.
sun	The **star** that other **celestial bodies** in a **solar system orbit**.
Sun	The star that is the source of light and heat for our solar system.
sun sign	The **zodiac constellation** that the **Sun** appears to be in at sunrise.
supersaturated solution	A **solution** that has more **solute** than is normally possible.
surface tension	The attraction between molecules at the surface of a liquid.
synthetic	Man-made.

tapered	Gradually narrower toward the end.
thermoplastic	A plastic that can be melted and re-formed over and over.
total solar eclipse	When the Moon comes between Earth and the **Sun** and blocks the light of the Sun completely.
transparent	The property of a material being so clear that light passes straight through it without changing the direction of the light; see-through.
transpiration	The release of water from the surface of a plant's leaves.
transpiration rate	A measure of **transpiration** in a given time.
tropics	A band about 3,000 miles (4,800 km) wide around the equator.
tropism	The response of a plant to a **stimulus**.
turgor	The firmness of cells due to the pressure of their contents on the cell **membrane**.
variable	Anything that can change on its own or be changed by you; changing.
vascular plant	A plant that has special tubes for transporting **sap**.
vegetative reproduction	The **cloning** of a plant.
velocity	The speed of an object moving in a certain direction.
vertical	A direction that is perpendicular to the horizon, which is an up/down position.
vibrate	To move back and forth.
viscosity	The measurement of a fluid's ability to flow; the measurement of fluid friction.
visible light	Light that the human eye can see.
visible radiation	The light that you can see.
visible spectrum	The different types of **visible light** listed in order of their energy.
vulcanization	The process of treating rubber with heat and sulfur.
waning	In reference to the Moon, it is the part of a **lunar month** when the moon phases get smaller each day.
water cycle	The process by which water moves back and forth between the Earth and the **atmosphere**.
waxing	In reference to the Moon, it is the part of a **lunar month** when the **moon phases** get bigger each day.
weather	The condition of the atmosphere in a region over a short period of time.
weathering	The process by which rocks are broken into smaller pieces.
white light	Light made of all the colors in the **visible spectrum**.
wind	The **horizontal** flow of air relative to Earth's surface.
work	The transfer of energy expressed as the product of the force and the distance through which it moves an object in the direction of that force.
xylem tube	Tubes that transport water and nutrients taken in through the roots throughout a plant.
zenith	The point in the sky that is directly overhead.
zodiac	The narrow band of sky on either side of the **ecliptic**.
zodiac constellation	A **constellation** associated with the **zodiac**.

Index